"Protagoras" and "Meno"

A volume in the series
Agora Editions
General Editor: Thomas L. Pangle
Founding Editor: Allan Bloom
A full list of titles in the series
appears at the end of the book.

PLATO
"Protagoras" *and "Meno"*

TRANSLATED, WITH
NOTES AND INTERPRETIVE ESSAYS, BY

ROBERT C. BARTLETT

Cornell University Press

ITHACA AND LONDON

First published 2004 by Cornell University Press
First printing, Cornell Paperbacks, 2004

Printed in the United States of America

Library of Congress Cataloging-in-Publication Data

Plato.
  [Protagoras, English]
  Protagoras ; and Meno / translated with notes and interpretive essays by Robert C.
Bartlett,—1st ed.
    p. cm.
Includes bibliographical references.
  ISBN 978-0-8014-4199-8 (cloth ; alk. paper) — ISBN 978-0-8014-8865-8 (pbk. ; alk. paper)
  1. Socrates.   2. Protagoras.   3. Sophists (Greek philosophy).   4. Ethics.   5. Virtue.
I. Bartlett, Robert C., 1964–   II. Plato. Meno. English.   III. Title.
  B382.A5B37   2004
  170—dc22

                                                                    2003020777

Cornell University Press strives to use environmentally responsible suppliers and
materials to the fullest extent possible in the publishing of its books. Such materials
include vegetable-based, low-VOC inks and acid-free papers that are recycled,
totally chlorine-free, or partly composed of nonwood fibers.
For further information, visit our website at www.cornellpress.cornell.edu.

Cloth printing   10   9   8   7   6   5   4   3   2   1
Paperback printing   10   9   8   7   6   5   4   3

Contents

Preface

This volume contains new translations of Plato's *Protagoras* and *Meno*, together with explanatory notes and interpretive essays. In preparing the translations, I assumed that Plato was a genuine philosopher who as such chose every word with "great exactness and exceeding precision," and I felt duty-bound to convey those choices as accurately as possible. In practice this means that I strove for the highest degree of literalness compatible with English style. Others before me have stated powerfully the case for literal translations, and over the course of the last generation such translations have begun to regain the place of honor they held in the Middle Ages, when William of Moerbeke, Henricus Aristippus, and Hunain ibn Ishaq, among others, painstakingly conveyed the thought of their Greek masters by means of literal translations. Let it suffice to say that the rather loose renderings typical of the last century, while perhaps more elegant or artful than their literal counterparts, ultimately frustrate the serious reader's attempt to track the nuances in argument and action characteristic of the Platonic dialogue.

In the present case I have attempted to translate consistently not only all terms of obvious philosophic importance (justice, courage, wisdom, piety, moderation, virtue, soul) but also such dramatic details as oaths and terms of address, which admittedly sound peculiar to our ears. Yet to follow previous translators in rendering "*Nē Dia*" ("By Zeus"), for example, as "good God" or "by heavens" or "for heaven's sake," needlessly conceals from readers the speaker's emphatic recourse to the greatest of the Greek gods (as distinguished from Hera or Apollo, to say nothing of Socrates' idiosyncratic oaths to a dog) and imports the familiar but misleading notions of God and heaven. In thus making Plato apparently more "accessible," one in fact pushes him still farther away.

Similarly, I have tried to attend to what might appear to be the smallest of Plato's literary choices. For example, almost all the available English translations of the *Protagoras* label Socrates' unnamed interlocutor a "friend," despite the fact that Plato identifies him as *hetairos* ("comrade" or "companion") rather than *philos*, the term usually and properly rendered as "friend." What is the significance of this difference? Whereas *philos* implies genuine intimacy between Socrates and his interlocutor, the much more ambiguous *hetairos*, with its suggestion of membership in a political club or party, need not. Students of recent political history will recall the phrase "Comrade, you are under arrest!" And the opening scene of the dialogue explains Plato's choice: the "comrade" proves to be more interested in gossip of a certain kind than philosophy, is thoroughly conventional in his deference to Homer and in his preference for the homegrown over the foreign, and travels less in the philosophical circles of Athens than does even young Hippocrates. What is more, Socrates' narration of the rest of the dialogue is directed to, and hence as it were filtered through, this "comrade": we ought not to expect Socrates to be as frank with such a fellow as he would be to a true friend, to a *philos* (consider *Republic* 450d10–e1), a fact one must keep in mind in reading all that follows.

The pairing of the *Protagoras* with the *Meno* is of course not the only one possible. With its repeated references to Gorgias, the *Meno* might well be linked with the dialogue named after that famous rhetorician, just as the *Protagoras* continues the report of Socrates' relations with Alcibiades begun in *Alcibiades I* and *II* (and completed in the *Symposium*) and so may be profitably read together with them. Yet the *Protagoras* ends with and culminates in the question "what is virtue?" (361c2–5), the very question that is the focus of the *Meno*, and Protagoras himself is mentioned prominently there as a preeminent teacher of virtue (*Meno* 91d3 and context). It is then the presence in both dialogues of the all-important question concerning virtue and its teachability that speaks in favor of reading them together.

For the *Protagoras*, I have used the text of Alfred Croiset in his edition of the works of Plato, prepared in collaboration with Louis Bodin: Platon, *Oeuvres complètes* vol. 3, pt. 1, *Protagoras* (Paris: Société d'édition "Les Belles Lettres," 1984 [1923]), although I have also consulted the following editions, commentaries, and philological studies: J. Adam and A. M. Adam, eds., *Protagoras*, 2d ed. (Cambridge: Cambridge University Press, 1921 [1905]); John Burnet, ed., *Opera Omnia Platonis*, vol. 3 (Oxford: Oxford University Press,

1983 [1903]); Bernd Manuwald, ed., *Protagoras* (Göttingen: Vandenhoeck & Ruprecht, 1999); Hermann Sauppe, ed., *Protagoras,* trans. James A. Towle (Boston: Ginn, 1892); W. J. Verdenius, "Bemerkungen zur Einleitung des *Protagoras*" in *Studia Platonica,* ed. Klaus Döring and Wolfgang Kullmann (Amsterdam: B. R. Grüner, 1974). The essay on the *Protagoras* first appeared, in somewhat different form, as "Political Philosophy and Sophistry: An Introduction to Plato's *Protagoras*" in *American Journal of Political Science* 47 (4): 612–24, reprinted with permission of the Midwest Political Science Association (© 2003 Midwest Political Science Association).

For the *Meno,* I have again used the text of Alfred Croiset, prepared in collaboration with Louis Bodin: Platon, *Oeuvres complètes,* vol. 3, pt. 2, *Gorgias et Ménon* (Paris: Société d'édition "Les Belles Lettres," 1992 [1923]). In addition, the following editions or commentaries proved useful: R. S. Bluck, *Plato's Meno* (Cambridge: Cambridge University Press, 1964); John Burnet, *Opera Omnia Platonis,* vol. 3 (Oxford: Clarendon Press, 1903); Jacob Klein, *A Commentary on Plato's Meno* (Chicago: University of Chicago Press, 1989 [1965]); R. W. Sharples, *Plato's Meno* (Chicago: Bolchazy-Carducci, 1985); E. Seymer Thompson, *The Meno of Plato* (New York and London: Garland, 1980 [1901]); and M. J. Verdenius, "Notes on Plato's *Meno,*" in *Mnemosyne* 10 (1957): 289–99. All materials contained in square brackets, as well as the geometrical diagrams that appear between 82c–85d, are not present in the original. The essay on the *Meno* first appeared, in somewhat different form, as "Socratic Political Philosophy and the Problem of Virtue" in *American Political Science Review* 93 (3): 525–33, reprinted with permission of Cambridge University Press.

Works referred to in the notes are by Plato unless otherwise indicated. The standard Stephanus pagination in the margins of both translations follows as closely as possible the edition of John Burnet.

I am grateful to the John M. Olin Foundation for a Junior Faculty Fellowship that gave me the freedom to begin this project and to the Earhart Foundation for a generous summer grant that enabled me to complete it. Thomas L. Pangle offered essential criticism and encouragement early on, and Peter Ahrensdorf, David Bolotin, Timothy Burns, Susan Collins, Judd Owen, and Andrew Patch offered suggestions on portions of the manuscript. My greatest debt is to Christopher Bruell, with whom I first studied Plato. I alone am responsible for the inadequacies in translation and interpretation that undoubtedly remain.

R. C. B.

Atlanta, Georgia

"Protagoras" and "Meno"

Protagoras
(Or, Sophists)[1]

DRAMATIS PERSONAE: COMRADE, SOCRATES

309a COMRADE: From where, Socrates, are you making your appearance? Or is it indeed clear that you're back from the hunt after Alcibiades[2] in his bloom? You know he appeared to me, when I saw him just the other day, to be a man who's beautiful[3] still—but a man for all that, Socrates, speaking just between ourselves, at least: he is already getting a full beard!

SOCRATES: What of it? Aren't you a praiser of Homer, who asserted[4]
309b that the most gracious time of life belongs to one who is getting his beard, the age Alcibiades is now?

COMRADE: So how do things stand now? Are you making your appearance, just back from him? And how is the young fellow disposed toward you?

1. It is uncertain whether the subtitles accompanying the dialogues are Plato's own or were added later, perhaps by the Hellenistic critic Thrasylus. For the case that the subtitles date from the fourth century B.C., and may well be Plato's own, see R. G. Hoerber, "Thrasylus' Platonic Canon and the Double Titles," *Phronesis* 2:10–20.
2. Alcibiades was to become one of the most colorful and controversial political figures of antiquity; for his exploits in the Peloponnesian War, in the course of which he aided the Athenians, Spartans, and Persians, see Thucydides 6–8 and Xenophon, *Hellenica* 1.1–2.2. Plato details Alcibiades' relations with Socrates in three additional dialogues: *Alcibiades I, Alcibiades II,* and *Symposium* (see also Xenophon, *Memorabilia* 1.2.12–47).
3. Or, "noble" (*kalos*). The word denotes both physical and moral beauty; it will be translated as "noble" ("nobly"), "beautiful" ("beautifully").
4. Homer, *Iliad* 24.348; *Odyssey* 10.279.

SOCRATES: Well disposed, in my opinion at least, and especially so today, for he said much on my behalf and came to my aid. And in fact I have just now come from him.

But I'm willing to tell you something strange: though he was present, not only did I not pay attention to him, I often even forgot about him.

309c COMRADE: And how could so great a thing[5] have happened between you and him? For no doubt you haven't come across anyone else more beautiful than he is, at least not in this city?

SOCRATES: I have, even much more so.

COMRADE: What are you saying? Is he a local or a foreigner?

SOCRATES: A foreigner.

COMRADE: From where?

SOCRATES: From Abdera.[6]

COMRADE: And some foreigner was so beautiful in your opinion that he appeared to you more beautiful than the son of Cleinias?

SOCRATES: How, you blessed one, won't that which is wisest appear more beautiful?

COMRADE: What! You're here with us, Socrates, just back from having met up with someone wise?

309d SOCRATES: No doubt the wisest of men nowadays—if in your opinion the wisest is Protagoras.

COMRADE: Oh! What are you saying? Protagoras has come to town?

SOCRATES: This is already his third day.

COMRADE: And you're back from having been with him just now?

310a SOCRATES: Yes, indeed; I said and heard many things.

COMRADE: Why then not relate to us the get-together, if nothing prevents your doing so? Sit down over here; just get the slave there to move up out of his seat.

SOCRATES: Certainly. And I'll be grateful, if you[7] listen.

COMRADE: And we to you, if you speak.

SOCRATES: The gratitude would be double. So listen.

In the course of this past night, when morning had not quite broken, Hippocrates, the son of Apollodorus and brother of Phason, be-
310b gan knocking very hard at my door with his walking stick. When

---

5. The word (*pragma*) has a range of meanings, from "matter" or "affair" to "thing," in the sense of a concrete reality, to "thing of consequence" or that which is an object of concern.
6. A prosperous Greek city on the coast of Thrace.
7. The plural "you."

someone opened the door for him, he immediately came barging in and, speaking in a loud voice, said, "Socrates, are you awake or asleep?"

I recognized his voice and said, "Hippocrates . . . there you are. No bad news to report, is there?"

"Nothing," he said, "but good things!"

"May what you say indeed be good," I said. "What is it, and for the sake of what have you arrived at this hour?"

"Protagoras has come," he said, standing alongside me.

"The day before yesterday," I said. "But you've just now learned of it?"

"Yes, by the gods," he said, "yesterday evening!" As he did so he 310c felt for my cot with his hand, sat down by my feet, and said, "Yes, yesterday evening, when I arrived very late in the day from Oenoe.[8] For you see, my slave Satyrus ran away from me, and though I intended to tell you that I was chasing after him, I forgot to because something else came along. Once I'd come back and we had dined and were about to retire, then it was that my brother tells me that Protagoras has come. And right then I undertook to go to you immediately, but I was of the opinion that it was much too late at night. But 310d just as soon as I'd slept off my exhaustion, I got up right away and began to make my way here!"

And I, recognizing his courage[9] and impetuosity, I said, "What's this to you? Surely Protagoras hasn't done you any injustice?"

And he said with a laugh, "Yes, by the gods, Socrates! Because he alone is wise but doesn't make me such!"

"But by Zeus," I said, "if you should give him money and persuade him, he'll make you wise too."

"Zeus and the gods!" he said. "If it were just a matter of that, I 310e wouldn't leave untouched anything of either my own things or what belongs to my friends. But it's on these very points that I've come now to you—to get you to have a conversation with him on my behalf—in part because I'm too young, in part because I've never even seen Protagoras or heard him at all: I was still a boy when he came to town before.[10] But, Socrates, all praise the man and assert that he is

---

8. A region near Eleutherae, on the way to Thebes. Evidently Hippocrates' escaped slave was making a run for Boeotian territory.

9. Or, "manliness" (*andreia*).

10. Or, "the first time."

wisest at speaking. So why don't we walk over to him, to catch him
311a while he's in? He's staying with Callias,[11] son of Hipponicus, as I
heard. So let's go!"

And I said, "Let's not go there yet, good one, for it's early. Instead
let's get up and go into the courtyard here, where we'll pass the time
strolling about until daylight. Then let's go. For Protagoras spends
most of his time indoors, so, not to worry, we'll catch him in, in all
likelihood."

After this we stood up and strolled about the courtyard. And to
311b make a test of Hippocrates' resolve, I began to examine him by asking: "Tell me, Hippocrates," I said, "you are now attempting to go to
Protagoras and intend to pay him money for his fee on your own behalf, on the grounds that you will go to whom and become what? Just
as if you had it in mind to go to your namesake Hippocrates the
Cosian, one of the Asclepiads,[12] and to pay him money for his fee on
your own behalf, and someone were to ask you: 'Tell me, Hip-
311c pocrates, you intend to pay a fee to Hippocrates on the grounds that
he is what?'—what would you answer?"

"I would say," he said, "'On the grounds that he is a physician.'"

"And so that you'll become what?"

"A physician," he said.

"And if you had it in mind to go to Polycleitus the Argive or Pheidias the Athenian[13] to pay their fee on your own behalf, and someone were to ask you: 'You have it in mind to pay this money to
Polycleitus and Pheidias on the grounds that they are what?'—what
would you answer?"

"I would say, 'On the grounds that they're sculptors.'"

"And so that you would become what?"

"That's clear—a sculptor."

311d "Well, then," I said, "in going now to Protagoras, you and I, we'll

---

11. Callias was the scion of a very wealthy and prominent Athenian family and was dogged
by controversy (see Andocides, *On the Mysteries* 124–27, for the unorthodox nature of Callias' private life). Xenophon and Plato present him as spending lavish amounts on sophists
in general and on Protagoras in particular (see *Cratylus* 391b–c; *Apology of Socrates* 20a;
Xenophon, *Symposium* 1.5).

12. That is, a physician. Hippocrates was by far the most famous physician in antiquity, after whom our Hippocratic oath is named (see also *Phaedrus* 270c–d).

13. Polycleitus of Argos was a leading sculptor in the second half of the fifth century B.C.,
best known for his depictions of athletes. Pheidias of Athens was probably the most celebrated sculptor of his day, whose works adorned the Parthenon.

be ready to pay him money for his fee on your behalf, if our money is sufficient and we persuade him with it; if not, we'll pay what belongs to our friends as well. If, then, someone should ask us, who are so exceedingly zealous about this, 'Tell me, Socrates and Hippocrates, you have it in mind to pay Protagoras money on the grounds that he is what?'—what answer would we give him? What other name do we hear spoken of Protagoras? Just as we hear 'sculptor' about Pheidias and 'poet' about Homer, so what sort of thing do we hear about Protagoras?"

311e

"Well, 'sophist' is what they call the man, at least, Socrates," he said.

"We are going then with the intention of paying money on the grounds that he is a sophist?"

"Absolutely."

"If then someone should ask you this in addition: 'You're going to Protagoras so that you yourself will become what?'"

312a

He blushed—for dawn had just broken, so that he became distinctly visible—and he said, "If it's at all like the previous things, it's clear—so that I'll become a sophist."

"And you," I said, "in the name of the gods, wouldn't you be ashamed to present yourself to the Greeks as a sophist?"

"Yes, by Zeus, Socrates, if I must say what I really think."

"But, Hippocrates, perhaps you don't suppose that the instruction Protagoras offers you will be of this sort but rather will be like that gained from the teacher of letters and the citharist[14] and the physical trainer? For you didn't learn each subject from these for the sake of the art—so that you'd become a skilled practitioner of them—but rather for the sake of such an education as befits an amateur[15] and a free man."

312b

"In my opinion the instruction Protagoras offers," he said, "is very much more of this sort."

"Do you know, then, what it is you are now about to do, or does it escape you?" I said.

"What's that?"

"That you are about to entrust your own soul to the care of a man who is, as you assert, a sophist. But I'd be filled with wonder if you

312c

14. The cithara was a plucked instrument with a U-shaped frame and tortoiseshell back.
15. Or, "layman" (*idiōtēs*): one who is not a skilled practitioner or professional (*dēmiourgos*).

know what in the world a sophist is. Yet if you are ignorant about this, you know neither to whom you are handing over your soul, nor whether you do so to something good or bad."

"I *think*, at least, that I know," he said.

"Then say it: what do you believe the sophist to be?"

"I believe him to be—just as the name implies—a knower of wise[16] things."

"Surely it's possible to say this about both painters and carpenters, that they are knowers of wise things. But if someone should ask us, 'Of what among the wise things are painters knowers?' we would say to him, I suppose, that they are such of things pertaining to the production of images, and so on with the others. But if someone should ask, 'The sophist is a knower[17] of what among the wise things?'— what would we answer him? At what sort of activity is he an expert?"[18]

"What could we say that he is, Socrates, except an expert at making one clever[19] at speaking?"

"Perhaps," I said, "we would speak truthfully, and yet not adequately. For our answer raises a further question: about *what* does the sophist make one clever at speaking? Just as the citharist no doubt makes one clever at speaking about what he also makes one a knower of—namely cithara playing. Is that so?"

"Yes."

"Well, then. About what does the sophist make one clever at speaking? Or is it clear that it would be about what he[20] also knows?"[21]

"That's likely, at any rate."

"So what is this about which the sophist himself is a knower and makes his student such as well?"

312d

312e

16. The phrase "wise things" (*ta sopha*) is related to the word "sophist" (*sophistēs*).

17. The phrase translated "is a knower" does not appear in the Greek but should probably be assumed from the preceding sentence. The Greek as it stands could be rendered: "The sophist is what among the wise?"

18. The word "expert" (or "overseer") (*epistatēs*) bears some resemblance to the word for "knower" (*epistēmōn*).

19. The word generally translated as "clever" (*deinos*) has a range of meanings, from skillful or clever, in its most positive form, to that which is terrible or frightening, as in the discussion of courage later in the dialogue, to that which is wondrous or strange. It is rendered as "terrific" at 339a.

20. The reading of three principal mss., followed by Croiset. Burnet reads the emendation of Stahl that translates as follows: "Or is it clear that it would be about what he also makes one a knower of?"

21. Reading Croiset's text; Burnet gives the last sentence here, in the form of a statement rather than a question, to Hippocrates and the next two to Socrates.

"By Zeus," he said, "I'm unable to tell you anything further."

313a   After this I said, "What then? Do you know what sort of a risk it is to which you intend to subject your soul? Or if you had to turn your body over to someone and run the risk of its becoming either useful[22] or worthless, you would have made every inquiry as to whether or not you should turn it over and would call on both friends and relatives for advice, investigating the matter for many days. But as for that which you believe to be worth more than the body, namely the soul, on whose usefulness or worthlessness depends whether all your own affairs fare well or badly—about this you've communicated with neither father nor brother nor any one of us who are your

313b   comrades as to whether or not you should turn your soul over to this newly arrived foreigner. Instead, you heard about him last evening, as you say, and have come at dawn, but you make no argument nor take any advice as to whether or not you should turn yourself over to him and instead are ready to spend both your own money and that of your friends, as though you already knew well that it is absolutely necessary to get together with Protagoras, whom you neither know,

313c   as you say, nor have ever conversed with. And you call him a sophist, but you are manifestly ignorant of what in the world the sophist is, to whom you are going to turn yourself over."

And when he heard this, he said, "It seems so, Socrates, on the basis of what you say."

"Well, then, Hippocrates, does the sophist happen to be a kind of wholesaler or retailer of the wares by which a soul is reared? For to me, at least, he appears to be something of this sort."

"And by what, Socrates, is a soul reared?"

"Doubtless by learning," I said. "And see to it, comrade, that the sophist, in praising what he has for sale, doesn't deceive us as do those who sell the nourishment of the body, the wholesaler and re-

313d   tailer. For they themselves too, I suppose, don't know what among the wares they peddle is useful or worthless to the body—they praise everything they have for sale—and neither do those who buy from them, unless one happens to be an expert physical trainer or a physician. So too those who hawk learning from city to city, selling and retailing it to anyone who desires it at any given moment: they praise all the things they sell. But perhaps some of these as well, best one, are ignorant of what among the things they sell is useful or worthless

---

22. Or, "good," "serviceable" (*chrēstos*).

313e   to the soul. And so too are those who buy from them, unless one happens to be a physician expert in what pertains to the soul.

"If, then, you happen to be a knower of what among these things is useful and worthless, it's safe for you to buy learning both from Protagoras and from anyone else whatever. But if not, blessed one,

314a   see that you do not roll the dice and run risks with the dearest things. For there is indeed much greater risk in the purchase of learning than there is in that of foods: it's possible to buy food and drink from the retailer and wholesaler and to take them off in other containers; and it's possible, before taking them into the body by drinking or eating them, to set them down at home and take counsel by calling upon someone knowledgeable as to what one should eat or drink and what one shouldn't and how much and when. As a result, the risk involved

314b   in the purchase isn't great. But it isn't possible to carry off learning in another container. Instead, for one who has paid the tuition and taken the instruction into the soul itself through having learned it, he necessarily goes off having already been harmed or benefited thereby.

"So let's also examine these things together with our elders, for we are still young to decide so great a matter. But now, since we're already under way, let's go and listen to the man and then, after we've listened, let's consort also with others. For Protagoras is not the only

314c   one there, but Hippias the Elean[23] is too—I think Prodicus the Cean[24] is as well—and many other wise men besides."

Since this seemed best to us, we began to make our way. But when we got to the porch, we stood there and continued to discuss a certain argument that had come up between us along the way. So as not to leave it incomplete, but to bring it to a conclusion and then enter, we stood on the porch conversing until we came to agreement with each other. Now in my opinion the porter, a certain eunuch, was overhearing us, and it's likely that he was annoyed by the frequent entries

314d   into the house, on account of the number of sophists there. At any rate, when we knocked on the door, he opened it and said upon see-

23. Hippias was among the most famous sophists in antiquity, known also for his involvement in political and diplomatic affairs. Plato devotes two dialogues to Socrates' conversations with him, the *Hippias Major* and *Hippias Minor* (see also Xenophon, *Memorabilia* 4.4.5–25).
24. The sophist Prodicus was best known for his precise use of language, as here in the *Protagoras*. Like most sophists, he charged very high fees for his classes: Socrates was able to attend the one drachma version of Prodicus' course, but not the fifty drachma one (*Cratylus* 384b; see also Xenophon, *Memorabilia* 2.1.21–34).

ing us, "Ugh! Sophists! He's[25] not at leisure!" At this he slammed the
door with both hands as hard as he could.

We began to knock again and, through the locked door, he said in
response: "You people![26] Didn't you hear that he's not at leisure?"

"But, good one," I said, "we haven't come for Callias, and neither
314e   are we sophists. So not to worry: we've come because we need to see
Protagoras. Please announce us." At length the fellow finally opened
the door for us.

Once inside, we came upon Protagoras walking about in the portico. And walking right along with him were, on the one side, Callias
315a   son of Hipponicus, his maternal half-brother Paralus son of Pericles,
and Charmides son of Glaucon;[27] on the other side were the other son
of Pericles, named Xanthippus, Philippides son of Philomelus, and
Antimoerus the Mendaean,[28] the one who is the most highly regarded of Protagoras' students and who is learning the art in order
to become a sophist himself. Of those who followed along behind
them listening to what was being said, the majority appeared to be
foreigners. These Protagoras brings from each of the cities he passes
315b   through, bewitching them with his voice like Orpheus,[29] and they in
their bewitched state follow his voice. There were also some natives
in the chorus. For my part, I was especially delighted at seeing this
chorus because they were taking noble precautions never to be in Protagoras' way by getting in front of him. Instead, when he himself and

---

25. That is, the porter's master, Callias.

26. Literally, "Human beings!" (*anthrōpoi*). The word can simply designate the human race
(as distinguished from animals or gods, for example) but can be a term of disparagement:
better to be a real man (*anēr*) or a gentleman (*kaloskagathos*) than a mere *anthrōpos*. It will be
translated as "human being" ("human beings"), "person" ("people"), or (at 314e, 330d, 334c,
and 338c) "fellow."

27. Pericles was the foremost Athenian statesman of his day, the leader of the democracy
when it began to wage the Peloponnesian War in 431 B.C.. Both he and his two sons are said
to have died in 429 B.C. as a result of the plague that befell Athens; Paralus is mentioned
also at *Alcibiades I* 118e and *Meno* 94b, Xanthippus at *Meno* 94b. Charmides was the uncle of
Plato and a promising student of Socrates: see *Symposium* 222b, *Theages* 128b, and the
Charmides as a whole, as well as Xenophon, *Memorabilia* 3.6.1 and 3.7.1–9, and *Symposium*
2.19, 3.1, 4.8, 27, 29–33. Like Alcibiades and Critias (n. 37), Charmides went on to have a
controversial career in politics: he was among the "Thirty Tyrants," the pro-Spartan oligarchs installed in Athens at the conclusion of the Peloponnesian War.

28. Philippides was a member of a wealthy Athenian family; nothing is known of Antimoerus.

29. A mythical singer able to charm with his music. He is perhaps best known for his journey to the underworld to retrieve his wife Eurydice, which he was permitted to do on condition that he not look at her until they returned; see *Symposium* 179d.

those with him turned around, the listeners nicely managed to split apart on both sides while maintaining their order, and, going around in a circle, they always went most beautifully to their places in the back.

315c "After him, I noticed,"[30] as Homer said, Hippias the Elean, sitting in an elevated chair in the portico opposite. Seated around him on stools were Eryximachus son of Acoumenus and Phaedrus the Myrrhinusian, as well as Andron son of Androtion and certain foreigners, some of whom were his fellow citizens, others not.[31] They appeared to be closely questioning Hippias concerning certain points in astronomy pertaining to nature and the things aloft, and he, seated in his chair, was rendering his judgment to each of them and going through their questions in detail.

315d "And I espied Tantalus too"[32]—for Prodicus the Cean was visiting as well. He was in a certain room that Hipponicus had used previously for storage but that now, on account of the number of the lodgers, Callias had emptied out and made into lodgings for the foreigners. Prodicus was still lying down, wrapped up in some sheepskins and very many bedclothes, as it appeared. Reclining alongside him on the neighboring couches were Pausanias of Cerameis and, with Pausanias, a lad still quite young, one noble and good[33] as regards his nature, I think, and certainly very beautiful in appearance.
315e I heard, I believe,[34] that his name is Agathon, and I wouldn't wonder if he happens to be Pausanias' beloved.[35] So there was this young lad, and both of the two Adeimantuses—one the son of Cepis,[36] the other the son of Leucolphidas[37]—and certain others made an appearance

---

30. Homer, *Odyssey* 11.601. Odysseus here mentions the next person he sees (Heracles) in his famous journey through the underworld.
31. Eryximachus, a physician, appears in the *Symposium* (and is mentioned at *Phaedrus* 268a); Phaedrus, of the Athenian deme or neighborhood Myrrhinus (see Verdenius ad loc.), appears in the *Phaedrus* and *Symposium*. Andron was one of the oligarchic Four Hundred who came to power for a short time in Athens in 411 B.C. (see also *Gorgias* 487c, where he is said to share the view that philosophizing to the point of precision is harmful).
32. Homer, *Odyssey* 11.582.
33. "Noble" and "good" are the two elements of the formula often translated as "gentleman" (*kaloskagathos*).
34. Elsewhere translated by one or more words related to "opinion" (*doxa/dokein*).
35. Pausanias appears again in the company of Agathon in the *Symposium*, the occasion for which is a party in honor of the latter's tragedy having taken first place in the Lenaea of 416 B.C. (see n. 81).
36. Otherwise unknown.
37. An active military leader under Alcibiades, this Adeimantus was captured at the battle of Aegospotami (405 B.C.) but was spared by the Spartans.

as well. But as for what they were conversing about, I for my part was unable to learn it because I was at some distance, eager though I was to hear Prodicus—in my opinion the man is altogether wise and di-

316a vine. But because his voice was deep, there was a kind of rumble in the room that was making what was being said unclear.

And we had just come in when Alcibiades the beautiful—as you say and as I am persuaded—came in behind us, as well as Critias[38] son of Callaeschrus. So once we were inside, we again passed time on a few small matters and, with them disposed of, we went over to Protagoras.

316b I said, "Protagoras, we've come to see you, you know, Hippocrates here and I."

"Do you wish," he said, "to converse with me alone, or together with the rest as well?"

"To us," I said, "it makes no difference. Once you've heard why we've come, you yourself consider it."

"What is it, then," he said, "that you've come for?"

"Hippocrates here is a native, a son of Apollodorus, of a great and prosperous house, and opinion has it that he himself is, as regards his nature, a match for those of his own age. In my opinion, he desires to

316c be held in high regard in the city, and he supposes that this will come to pass for him above all if he should associate with you. So now consider these things—whether you think you by yourself ought to converse about them with us by ourselves, or together with the rest."

"You correctly take forethought on my behalf, Socrates," he said. "For a man who is a foreigner and who goes into great cities and there persuades the best of the young to forsake the company of others— both kin and others, older and younger—and to associate with him, on the grounds that they will become the best possible through their

316d associating with him—the one who does these things must take precautions. For no little envy arises over these things, and other ill will and hostile plots as well.

"Now, I assert that the sophistic art is ancient and that those of the ancient men who practiced it fashioned, out of fear of the hostility

---

38. A sometime member of the Socratic circle and among its most controversial, Critias took part in the revolution of the Four Hundred oligarchs in Athens in 411 B.C. and was subsequently exiled after the restoration of the democracy. When Athens finally surrendered at the conclusion of the Peloponnesian War in 404 B.C., Critias returned from exile to become one of the ardently pro-Spartan "Thirty Tyrants" who ruled Athens with a brutal hand. See Xenophon, *Hellenica* 2.3–4, 15, 18, 24–56; 4.8–9, 19, and *Memorabilia* 1.2.12–39. He figures prominently in the *Charmides*.

arising from it, a cloak for themselves and wrapped themselves in it. For some this cloak was poetry—for example, Homer and Hesiod, · and Simonides—for others in turn, like Orpheus and Musaeus[39] and their followers, initiation rites and prophecies. And I've perceived certain others who've even used physical training—for example, Iccus[40] of Tarentum and that one who is still alive today and is inferior

316e   to no one as a sophist, Herodicus of Selymbria,[41] originally a Megarian. And your Agathocles[42] made use of music as a cloak for himself, though he was in fact a great sophist, as well as Pythocleides the Cean[43] and many others. All these, as I say, being afraid of envy, made use of these arts[44] as concealments.

317a   "But I don't concur with any of them in this. For I believe that they did not quite accomplish what they wished: they didn't escape the notice of those among humans with the power to act in the cities, for whose sake these cloaks exist. For the many, at any rate, perceive as it were nothing but instead just recite whatever the powerful proclaim. So for anyone who tries to run away in stealth but isn't able to

317b   do so and is clearly seen, even the attempt is very foolish, and it necessarily makes humans much more ill-disposed toward him. For they hold that such a person is, in addition to other things, a scoundrel as well.

"Now I have followed a path that is the complete opposite of theirs. I grant that I am a sophist and that I educate human beings, and I think this is a better precautionary measure than theirs, namely granting it rather than denying it. And I've considered other measures in addition to this, such that—to speak with god—I suffer noth-

317c   ing terrible on account of my granting that I am a sophist, though I've been engaged in the art for many years now and in fact all my years taken together are many—in point of age I could be the father of any one of you. So it would be much the most pleasant thing for me, if it's

39. A mythical singer best known for his oracular pronouncements; see *Apology of Socrates* 41a, *Ion* 536b, and *Republic* 363c and 364e, as well as Aristophanes, *Frogs* 1032–33. (For Orpheus, see n. 29.)

40. Iccus won the pentathlon in the Olympic Games and subsequently became a renowned trainer (*Laws* 839e–840a, as well as Pausanias 6.10.6).

41. See also *Phaedrus* 227d and *Republic* 406a–c.

42. Mentioned also at *Laches* 180d as the teacher of Damon, himself a famous teacher of music.

43. See also *Alcibiades I* 118c, where he is mentioned as having been the teacher of Pericles.

44. *Technai* (singular *technē*): any expertise, skill, or craft characterized by knowledge.

at all what you want, to fashion a speech[45] about these things before all these who are inside."

And I—for I suspected that he wanted to make a display before Prodicus and Hippias and to preen himself on the fact that we had
317d   come as his lovers—I said, "Why then don't we call over Prodicus and Hippias, and those with them, so they may hear us?"

"Certainly," Protagoras said.

"Do you want us, then, to arrange the gathering so that you may take your seats and converse?" Callias said.

That was held to be what was needed. We were all pleased because we were going to hear wise men, and we ourselves got hold of the stools and couches and arranged them by Hippias; the couches were already over there. In the meantime both Callias and Alcibiades had
317e   got Prodicus up out of bed and came over, the two of them leading Prodicus and those with him.

When we were all seated together, Protagoras said, "Now then, Socrates, since these here are present too, perhaps you might say what you were mentioning to me just a moment ago on behalf of the young fellow."
318a   And I said, "My beginning point is the same, Protagoras, as the one I made just now concerning why I've come. For Hippocrates here happens to be in the grip of a desire for your company. So he says that he would gladly learn what will result for him if he is together with you. Such was the extent of our speech."

Protagoras then said in response: "Well, young fellow, it will be possible for you, if you associate with me, on the day you do get together with me, to go home in a better state, and the same holds for the next day as well. In fact, every day you will continually take steps toward improvement."
318b   Having listened, I said, "Protagoras, what you're saying is nothing to be wondered at, but is likely. For if someone should teach even you, who are of such an age and so wise, what you might not happen to know, you would become better. But don't [answer][46] in this way. Instead, just as if Hippocrates here should very suddenly undergo a change in his desire and desire instead the company of that young

---

45. *Logos*. This important term will be translated as "speech," "argument," or "account," depending on the context.
46. In this not uncommon idiom, no main verb is explicit; a similar formulation occurs at *Meno* 74d.

fellow who's very recently visited, Zeuxippus[47] the Heraclean; and,
318c   in going to him as he has now to you, if he should hear from him these
same things he has from you—namely that every day he will become
better and improve because he associates with him—what if Hippocrates should ask him further: 'In what respect do you assert that
I will be better, and in regard to what will I improve?' then Zeuxippus would say to him, 'In painting.' And if in getting together with
Orthagoras[48] the Theban he heard from him these same things he has
from you, he should ask him in turn in what respect he will be better
day by day because of his getting together with him, he would say,
'In point of aulos[49] playing.' So now you too speak in this way to the
young fellow, and to me who am asking on his behalf, 'By getting to-
318d   gether with Protagoras, on the very day that he gets together with
him, Hippocrates here will go away in a better state and improve
every day thereafter—but improve in what respect, Protagoras, and
concerning what?'"

And Protagoras, having listened to these things from me, said,
"You ask in a noble manner, Socrates, and I delight in answering
those who ask in a noble manner. For by coming to me, Hippocrates
will not undergo what he would have done by getting together with
any of the other sophists: these other ones mistreat the young. For al-
318e   though the young have fled the arts, the other sophists lead them
against their will and plunge them back into the arts, teaching them
calculation and astronomy and geometry and music"—and as he
said this he cast a glance at Hippias. "But in coming to me he will
learn about nothing other than that for the sake of which he has come.
The subject in question is good counsel concerning one's own affairs—how he might best manage his own household—and, con-
319a   cerning the affairs of the city, how he might be the most powerful[50]
in carrying out and speaking about the city's affairs."

"Do I follow your argument?" I said. "For in my opinion you mean
the political art and you claim to make men good citizens."

"That is it, Socrates," he said, "the very profession I profess."

---

47. Almost certainly the same as Zeuxis of Heraclea: see Manuwald ad loc., as well as *Gorgias* 453c.
48. According to Athenaeus (*The Deipnosophists* 184e), Orthagoras taught Epaminondas to play the aulos.
49. The aulos was a reed instrument somewhat similar to the modern oboe.
50. Or, "the most capable" (*dunatōtatos*); compare 317a.

"It is to be sure a noble craft you possess," I said, "if in fact you do possess it—for nothing will be said to you, at least, apart from what I think. For I didn't suppose this to be something teachable, Protago-
319b ras, but I don't see how I might disbelieve you when you say that it is. Why I don't hold it to be something teachable, nor something that humans can bestow on other humans, it's just for me to explain. For I assert that Athenians are wise, as do the other Greeks. Now I see, when we gather together in the assembly, that whenever the city must carry out some matter pertaining to construction, the builders are sent for as advisors concerning the construction projects, and whenever concerning the building of ships, the shipwrights, and so on with all the other matters they hold to be subject to instruction and
319c teachable. But if someone else attempts to advise them whom they do not suppose to be a skilled practitioner, then, even if he is very beautiful and wealthy and from well-born stock, they are not at all receptive to him but ridicule him and make an uproar until either the one attempting to speak is shouted down and steps aside himself or the city police drag or carry him off at the bidding of the prytanes.[51]

"This, then, is how they act concerning those matters they suppose to be subject to an art. But whenever they must deliberate about
319d something pertaining to the city's management, a craftsman who stands up may advise them concerning these things, every bit as much as a blacksmith or cobbler, merchant or captain, rich man or poor, well- or low-born; and no one rebukes them for this, as in the previous cases, because one of them hasn't learned this anywhere or had any teacher but nonetheless attempts to give advice. For it's clear that they don't hold this to be something teachable.

"Not only is this the case concerning the common affairs of the city,
319e but in private too our wisest and best citizens aren't able to bestow on others that virtue which they possess. Pericles, the father of these young fellows here, educated them nobly and well in those matters that depend on teachers, but as for those things in regard to which he
320a himself is wise, he neither educates them himself nor gives them over to anyone else. Rather, they go around grazing unrestrained,[52] in the hopes that they might on their own stumble across virtue some-

---

51. That is, the officials presiding over the assembly (see also 338a).
52. The image is that of the "sacred cattle" allowed to graze at will around certain temples; see *Critias* 119d.

where. Take Cleinias, if you like, the younger brother of Alcibiades here. This same man, Pericles, is Cleinias' guardian,[53] and for fear that Cleinias might indeed be corrupted by Alcibiades, Pericles separated him from Alcibiades, settled him in the home of Ariphron, and educated him. And before six months were up, Ariphron gave him
320b back to Pericles because he was unable to handle him. And I can tell you of very many others who, though they are good themselves, have never yet made anyone better, either kinfolk or others. So I, Protagoras, in view of these things, don't hold virtue to be something teachable.

"But when I hear you saying this, I waver and think that what you say makes sense, on account of my belief that you are experienced in many things, have learned many things, and have discovered some yourself. So if you can make a more effective demonstration for us that virtue is something teachable, don't be begrudging but demon-
320c strate it."

"Well, Socrates," he said, "I won't begrudge it. But am I to make a demonstration to you,[54] as an older man to younger ones, by telling a myth or by going through an argument?"[55]

Many of those seated nearby replied to him that he should proceed in whatever way he wished. "Well, then," he said, "in my opinion it is more gratifying to tell you a myth.

"Once there was a time when there were gods but not mortal
320d species. But when the allotted time came for their coming into being as well, gods formed them in the earth by mixing together earth and fire and as many things as are compounds of fire and earth. And when they were about to lead them to the light, they commanded Prometheus and Epimetheus[56] to order and distribute powers to all severally, as appropriate. Epimetheus begged Prometheus to allow him to make the distributions, saying, 'After I've made the distribution, you examine it.' And having thus persuaded him, Epimetheus

---

53. The father of Cleinias and Alcibiades (Cleinias) fell in the battle at Coronea in 447 B.C. Pericles and his brother Ariphron then assumed guardianship of the boys (see, in general, Plutarch's *Life of Alcibiades*). For one telling example of Pericles' relationship with Alcibiades, consider Xenophon, *Memorabilia* 1.2.40–46. As for Alcibiades' opinion of his brother, see *Alcibiades I* 118e.
54. The plural "you."
55. *Mythos* and *logos* respectively.
56. Their names mean "forethought" and "afterthought" respectively. The verb related to "forethought" appears at 316c and 361d.

made his distributions. He did so by granting strength without speed
320e to some, on the one hand, and by adorning the weaker ones with
speed, on the other. To some he gave weapons; to those he gave an
unarmed nature, he contrived for them some other capacity[57] to preserve themselves. For to those he endowed with a small stature he
distributed winged escape or a subterranean dwelling; and to those
he increased in size, by that very provision he preserved them. And
321a so also with the rest he made his distributions in an equalizing way
and, taking precautions, he so contrived them that no one species
would be wiped out.

"Once he had provided them with a means of escape from their
mutual destruction, he contrived protection against the seasons that
come from Zeus, clothing them in thick hair and tough skin adequate
to guard against winter, on the one hand, and capable of doing so also
against scorching heat, on the other; and these same things provide
for them, when they go to sleep, a bedding belonging to and grow-
ing spontaneously[58] for each. And some he shod with hooves, others
321b with[59] tough and bloodless skin. He then made thorough provision
for their various means of nourishment: to some he gave the pasture
of the land, to others the fruits of trees, to still others roots. And there
are some to whom he gave other animals to be their fleshy suste-
nance, but these he made reproduce in small numbers, those con-
sumed by them in great numbers, thus providing for the preservation
of the species.

"Now since Epimetheus was not so wise, it escaped his notice that
321c he had entirely used up the capacities[60] on the nonrational beings.[61]
Indeed, the race of human beings still remained for him to order, and
he was perplexed as to how he might deal with them. Prometheus
then came to him in his perplexity in order to examine the distribution, and he saw the other animals suitably provided for in all
respects but mankind naked and unshod, without bedding and
weapons.

"But by now the allotted day was already at hand when mankind

---

57. Or, "power."
58. The root of the word this phrase translates (*autophuēs*) means in the first place to grow
(*phuō*) and hence is related also to the word for "nature" (*phusis*).
59. The mss. add at this point the phrase "hairs and," but it is rejected by the modern editors.
60. Or, "powers."
61. Literally, "the things without speech." The phrase is omitted in one principal ms.

had to go up out of the earth into the light. So Prometheus, being perplexed as to what means of preservation he might discover for 321d mankind, stole from Hephaestus and Athena their technical wisdom, together with fire—for there was no way for anyone to possess or make use of it without fire—and in this way he indeed bestowed a gift on mankind. Mankind, then, obtained by this means the wisdom pertaining to their livelihood,[62] but they did not have the political wisdom: that resided with Zeus.

"There was no longer time for Prometheus to enter the Acropolis, the dwelling of Zeus—and in addition, the guardians[63] of Zeus were 321e fearsome—but he did enter unnoticed into the common dwelling of Athena and Hephaestus, where the two of them practiced their art.[64] Having stolen both the fiery art of Hephaestus and the other art belonging to Athena,[65] he gave them to mankind. As a result of this, the livelihood of mankind is well provided for, but later on Prometheus, 322a thanks to Epimetheus, was prosecuted on a charge of theft, according to what is said.

"Since mankind had a share of the divine allotment, in the first place they believed in gods, alone among the animals, on account of their kinship with the god,[66] and they undertook to build both altars to and statues of gods. Second, they quickly formulated articulate speech and names, by means of art, and they invented for themselves dwellings and clothing and shoes and bedding and the nourishment from the earth.

"Having thus provided for themselves, human beings in the earli- 322b est times lived scattered about; there were no cities. They then perished at the hands of the wild beasts because they were in every respect weaker than they, and although their skillful art was an adequate aid for their nourishment, when it came to the war against wild beasts it was deficient: they did not yet have the political art, of which the art of war is a part. So they sought to gather themselves together and to preserve themselves by founding cities. But whenever they

62. Or, perhaps, "life" (*bios*).
63. Presumably Cratos and Bia ("Strength" and "Force"); see Hesiod, *Theogony* 385–88.
64. Literally, "loved their art." The verb is parallel to the verb to philosophize; literally, "to love wisdom."
65. Athena was regarded as the patron of the technical arts and crafts in general.
66. The phrase "on account of their kinship with the god" is questioned by several editors but is present in the mss. For a defense of it, see Robert Renehan, "Studies in Greek Texts," *Hypomnemata* 43 (1976): 123.

gathered together, they committed injustices against one another because they didn't have the political art and, as a result, they scattered once again and were in the process of being destroyed.

322c   "Now Zeus, fearing that our race might perish altogether, sent Hermes to bring shame[67] and justice to human beings in order that there might be principles of order in cities and unifying bonds of friendship. So Hermes asked Zeus in what manner, then, he should give justice and shame to human beings: 'As the arts have been distributed, so am I to distribute these as well? The arts have been distributed in the following way: one who possesses the medical art is sufficient for many laypersons, and so on with the other skilled practitioners. Am I to place justice and shame among human beings in
322d   this way, or am I to distribute them to all?' 'To all,' Zeus said, 'and let all have a share. For cities would not come into being if few should share in them as in other arts. And set it down as a law from me that he who is incapable of sharing in shame and justice is to be killed as an illness in a city.'

"So in this way and for these reasons, Socrates, not only the Athenians but the rest too suppose that few have a share in the giving of advice, whenever there is an argument pertaining to virtue in building or to that in some other skilled practice, and if someone apart
322e   from the few gives advice, they don't tolerate it—as you[68] assert; and as is only reasonable, as I assert. But whenever they proceed to advice having to do with political virtue, which must as a whole follow
323a   the path of justice and moderation, they reasonably tolerate it from *every* man on the grounds that it is proper for everyone to have a share in this virtue, at any rate, or else there won't be cities. That, Socrates, is the cause of this.

"And so that you don't suppose you're being deceived that all human beings really do believe that every man shares in justice and the rest of political virtue, take as an additional piece of evidence the following. For in the case of the other virtues, just as you say, if someone asserts that he is a good aulos player but isn't (or as regards any
323b   other art whatever), either they ridicule him or treat him harshly, and when his relatives approach him they admonish him as one who is mad. But as for justice and the rest of political virtue, even if they do

67. Or, "awe," "reverence" (*aidōs*).
68. The singular "you," here and throughout 328d (with the exceptions indicated in nn. 78 and 80).

know of someone that he is unjust, and if he himself tells the truth about himself before many, yet while in the former case they held telling the truth to be moderation,[69] in this they hold it to be madness and assert that all must *say* they are just, whether they are or not, and that anyone who doesn't pretend to possess justice is mad. They do so on the grounds that everyone should somehow or other share in

323c   it or cease to be among human beings. That they reasonably accept every man as an advisor concerning this virtue, then, on account of their belief that everyone has a share of it, I have these things to say.

"But that they don't believe it to be by nature or spontaneous, but rather something teachable and present in those in whom it is present as a result of diligence—this I'll try to demonstrate to you next. For no one becomes angry or admonishes or teaches or punishes those who possess any of the bad things that human beings believe

323d   their fellows possess by nature or through chance, in order that they not be such as they are. Rather, they pity them. For example, who is so thoughtless as to attempt to do any of these things to those who are ugly or small or weak? For they know, I think, that these things belong to human beings by nature and through chance—the noble things and their contraries.

"But as for all the goods that they suppose belong to human beings as a result of diligence and practice and teaching, if someone does not

323e   possess these but rather the bad things opposed to them, then it is against these, presumably, that anger and punishments and admonitions arise. One among these is injustice and impiety and, in a word,

324a   all that is opposed to political virtue. Then indeed everyone becomes angry at and admonishes anyone of this sort, clearly on the grounds that it can be acquired through diligence and learning.

"For if you're willing to reflect, Socrates, on what in the world punishing the unjust amounts to, it will teach you that human beings, at least, believe virtue to be something that can be readily provided. For no one punishes those who are unjust with his mind focused on the fact that they committed injustice and for that reason—unless some-

324b   body seeks retribution in an irrational way, like a wild beast. But one who attempts to punish in accord with reason seeks retribution not for the sake of the past act of injustice—that would not undo what

69. Or, "good sense," "clear-mindedness," "level-headedness" (*sōphrosunē*). The word will consistently be translated as "moderation," but as Socrates himself makes clear (332a–333b), it has a range of meanings.

has already been done—but for the sake of the future one, so that neither the criminal himself nor anyone else who sees him punished may commit injustice again.

"With such a thought in mind, he thinks virtue can be gained by education; at any rate it is for the sake of deterrence that he punishes. 324c All those, then, who seek retribution, both privately and publicly, have this opinion. Not only do other human beings seek retribution and exact punishment in the case of those they think are unjust, but so do the Athenians in particular, your fellow citizens. As a result, according to this account, Athenians too are among those who believe virtue to be something readily provided and teachable.

"That your fellow citizens reasonably accept political advice from a blacksmith and cobbler, and that they believe virtue to be something teachable and readily provided—these things have been ade- 324d quately demonstrated for you, Socrates, as it appears to me at least. There still remains the perplexity which puts you at a loss concerning the good men: why in the world do the good men teach their own sons and make them wise in all that depends on teachers, but, when it comes to that virtue with respect to which they themselves are good, they don't make them better than anybody else? About this, Socrates, I'll no longer tell you a myth but rather an argument. Reflect on the following.

"Is there or is there not some one thing that all citizens necessarily 324e share in, if in fact there is to be a city? For in this and in nothing else lies the resolution of the perplexity that puts you at a loss. For if there is, and this one thing is not the art of building or smithing or pottery, 325a but justice and moderation and being pious—that one thing I call the virtue of a man, to sum it up; if this is what all must share in, and with this every man who wants to learn or do anything else must act and without it must not, and if the one who doesn't share in this—child and man and woman—must be taught and punished until he becomes better by being punished and the one who doesn't pay heed 325b while being punished and taught must be cast out from the cities or killed on the grounds that he is incurable; if this is so, and given that it is such by nature, then if the good men teach their sons all else but not this, consider how much the good are to be wondered at.[70]

70. The reading of most modern editors. Burnet and Manuwald print the reading of the mss., which translates: "consider in how wondrous a way the good come into being."

"For that they believe it to be something teachable in both private and public, we have demonstrated. But although it is something teachable and can be cultivated, do they teach their sons all else, things for which there is no death penalty if they don't know them, yet fail to teach them and make every effort to be diligent about those things that, if their sons don't learn them and haven't been cultivated

325c   with a view to virtue, they are liable to the death penalty and banishment—and in addition to death, the confiscation of property and the all but utter undoing of house and home? One must suppose that they do, Socrates. Beginning from their earliest youth and continuing for so long as they are alive, [parents] both teach and admonish them. As soon as he understands the spoken word, nurse and mother and

325d   attendant and the father himself earnestly strive to see to it that the boy will be the best possible, teaching and demonstrating, with regard to every deed and speech, that one thing is just, another unjust; and that this is noble, that shameful; and that this is pious, that impious: 'Do these things!' 'Don't do those!' And if he willingly obeys,[71] [fine], but if not, then they straighten him out with threats and blows just as if he were warped and bent wood.

"After this they send him off to the teachers and enjoin them to be

325e   much more diligent about the good behavior of the boys than about letters and cithara playing. The teachers are indeed diligent about these things, and when in turn the students learn letters and are on the point of understanding the written word, just as before they understood the spoken word, the teachers set before them at their benches the works of good poets to read, and they compel the stu-

326a   dents to memorize them. Contained in these works are many admonitions and many detailed descriptions and praises and encomia of the good men of old, so that the boy, out of emulation, imitates them and longs to become such himself. The citharists too, in turn, are diligent in comparable ways about both moderation and seeing to it that the young do no wrong. In addition to these things, when they learn to play the cithara, the instructors teach in turn the works of yet other good lyric poets and, setting these to the music of the cithara, they

326b   compel the souls of the boys to make their own the rhythms and harmonies so that they may be gentler and, by becoming more rhythmic

---

71. Or, "is persuaded."

and harmonious, be serviceable[72] in point of speaking and acting. For human life as a whole requires good rhythm and harmony.

"And next, in addition to these things, they send them to a physical trainer so that, possessing better bodies, they may serve a mind 326c that is now serviceable[73] and will not be compelled to be cowards through the wretched condition of their bodies, both in wars and in other actions.

"Those who are especially powerful do this, and the wealthiest are especially powerful:[74] their sons begin to frequent the teachers at the earliest age and are released from them at the latest. And once they are released from the teachers, the city in turn compels them both to learn the laws[75] and to live in accordance with these as paradigms[76] 326d so that they may not act haphazardly according to their own inclinations. Rather, just as the writing teachers trace the letters with a stylus for those of the boys not yet skilled at writing and then give them the writing tablet and compel them to write according to the tracings of the letters, so also the city, having traced the laws that are the inventions[77] of good legislators of old, compels them both to rule and to be ruled in accord with these. Whoever ventures beyond them it punishes, and the name for this punishment among you,[78] and every- 326e where else, is 'correction,'[79] on the grounds that justice corrects. Given so great a diligence concerning virtue in both private and public, then, do you wonder, Socrates, and are you perplexed as to whether virtue is something teachable? But you shouldn't wonder— much more so if it *weren't* something teachable.

"On account of what, then, do many sons of good fathers become paltry? Learn this in turn. For it's nothing to be wondered at, if in fact what I was saying previously is true, that in this matter—in virtue— 327a no one should be an unskilled layman if there is to be a city. For if indeed what I say is so—and it is so above all else—choose any other

72. *Chrēstos*: see n. 22.
73. *Chrēstos*, as in n. 72.
74. The reading of the mss. Croiset and Burnet accept the emendation of Sauppe that would read: "Those who are especially powerful do this most of all."
75. Or, "customs," "legal conventions" (*nomoi*).
76. The phrase "as paradigms" (or "examples") is deleted by some editors but is present in the mss.
77. Or, "discoveries."
78. The plural "you."
79. The same verb is translated as "straighten out" at 325b.

practice and subject of learning whatever and reflect on it. If there couldn't be a city unless we all were aulos players (of whatever sort each of us was able to be), and everyone taught this to everyone else in both private and public and rebuked one who didn't play nobly and wasn't begrudging in this, just as at present no one is begrudg-
327b   ing or conceals anything when it comes to the just and lawful things, as they do in the case of other matters subject to an art—for, I think, reciprocal justice and virtue are profitable for you.[80] For these reasons everyone eagerly speaks to and teaches everyone else about the just and lawful things.

"So if in the case of aulos playing we had such all-out eagerness and unbegrudging generosity in teaching one another, do you suppose, Socrates," he said, "that the sons of the good aulos players would become good aulos players any more than those of the paltry ones? I don't think so, but whoever's son happened to have the best
327c   nature for aulos playing would grow to become renowned, and whoever's was without that nature would be without that fame. And many times a paltry one would issue from a good player, many times a good player from a paltry one. But they *all* would be competent aulos players in comparison with the unskilled laymen who are without any expertise in aulos playing".

"So suppose now that, whatever human being appears to you the most unjust among those reared under laws and amidst human beings, he is himself just and a skilled practitioner of this matter, should
327d   it be necessary to judge him in comparison with human beings who are without education or courts or laws or, in addition, any necessity always compelling them to be diligent about virtue. Rather, these latter would be like those savages whom Pherecrates the poet presented last year at the Lenaea.[81] Indeed, in being amidst such sorts of human beings, as were the misanthropes in that chorus, you'd be glad if you should come across Eurybatus and Phrynondas[82] and would cry out with longing for the wickedness of human beings here.

---

80. The plural "you," and the reading of the mss.; the modern editors, following Stephanus, read "for us."
81. Pherecrates was a successful Athenian comic playwright who won his first victories between 440 and 430 B.C. and produced *The Savages*—perhaps the play alluded to here—in 420 B.C. (Athenaeus, *The Deipnosophists* 218d). The Lenaea was a precinct sacred to Dionysus near both the Acropolis and the theater. The word came by extension to signify the festival celebrated there, an important part of which was the presentation of plays, tragedies as well as comedies.
82. Eurybatus was a notorious thief, Phrynondas a cheat and liar.

327e   "But as it is you are spoiled, Socrates, because all are teachers of
virtue, insofar as each is able, and none is apparent to you. Well, just
as if you should inquire who is a teacher of Greek, no single one
328a   would be apparent, nor would there be one, I think, if you should inquire who teaches for us the sons of manual laborers the very art that
they've in fact learned from their fathers—insofar as the father is able
to, as well as the father's friends in the same trade. It wouldn't be
easy, I think, Socrates, for a teacher to be apparent who might teach
them further, but it would be altogether easy for an instructor to be
apparent if he taught the inexperienced. And so it is with virtue and
all other things.

"But if there is someone among us who differs just a little in bring-
328b   ing about an advance toward virtue, that is something to be glad of.
Indeed, I think I am one of these and that I aid[83] someone's becoming noble and good better than do other human beings and that I am
worthy of the fee I charge and still more, as is the opinion even of the
student himself. For these reasons too I have fashioned a certain way
of charging my fee: whenever someone studies with me, he pays me
328c   the money I charge if he wants to; but if he doesn't want to he goes
into a temple, swears how much he asserts the teachings to be worth,
and puts down that much.

"Such, Socrates," he said, "is both the myth and the argument I
have for you, to the effect that virtue is something teachable and the
Athenians believe it to be such, and that it's nothing to be wondered
at if sons of the good fathers become paltry and sons of the paltry become good. For even the sons of Polycleitus,[84] who are of the same
age as Paralus and Xanthippus here, are nothing in comparison to
their father, and such is the case with other sons of other skilled prac-
328d   titioners. But there isn't yet reason to level this charge against these
fellows here, for there is still hope in their case: they are young."

Having made a display of this sort and length, Protagoras brought
his speech to a close. I was bewitched and was still looking over at
him for a long time because I thought he was going to say something
else, which I wanted to hear. But when I perceived that he really had
stopped, with difficulty I somehow gathered myself together, so to
speak, and said, looking toward Hippocrates: "Son of Apollodorus,

83. Reading Dobree's conjecture, *onēsai,* adopted by all modern editors, rather than the
reading of the mss., *noēsai* ("and that I notice someone with a view to their becoming").
84. See 311c. Perhaps in confirmation of Protagoras' point, nothing is now known of Polycleitus' sons.

how grateful I am to you for having urged me to come here. For I
328e   value having heard what I've heard from Protagoras. Previously I
used to hold that it is not through human diligence that the good become good, but now I've been persuaded.

"Except I do have a certain small obstacle that, it's clear, Protagoras will easily instruct us about as well, since he has also given thorough instruction about these many things. For if someone should get
together with any one of the popular speakers concerning these very
329a   matters, he would perhaps hear speeches of just this sort from either
Pericles or anyone else among those competent at speaking. But if he
should ask one of them something beyond that, then, like books, they
have nothing to say in reply or to offer as a question themselves. If,
however, someone asks them even something small concerning what
they've said, then like struck bronze that rings for a long time and
continues to do so unless someone touches it, so also the orators,
though they've been asked about small points, stretch out their
329b   speech to a very great length. And Protagoras here is capable of making long and beautiful speeches, as is clear, but he is capable also of
replying briefly when asked something and, when he asks a question,
to wait for and accept the answer, things given to few people.

"So now, Protagoras, it is a small thing I am in need of, in order to
have everything—if you could just answer me the following: you assert that virtue is something teachable, and if I were to be persuaded
by any human being, it would be by you. Just satisfy my soul about
329c   this point that I wondered about in what you said.

"For you were saying that Zeus sent justice and shame to human
beings, and in many places in your speeches it was said by you that
justice and moderation and piety and all these things were some one
thing taken together, namely virtue. So go through these very things
precisely for me by means of argument—that is, whether virtue is
some one thing, and justice and moderation and piety are parts of it;
or whether these things that I was just now speaking of are all names
329d   of it, it being one and the same thing. This is what I still desire."

"But that, at least, is easy to answer, Socrates," he said. "The things
you ask about are parts of virtue, which is one."

"Is it," I said, "just as the parts of the face are parts—mouth and
nose and eyes and ears—or as the parts of gold do not differ at all,
one from another or from the whole, except in respect to bigness or
smallness?"

329e   "The former appears to me, Socrates, to be the case—just as the parts of the face are in relation to the whole face."

"So," I said, "do human beings also partake of these parts of virtue, some of one part, others of another; or is it necessarily the case that if in fact someone lays hold of one, he has them all?"

"Not at all," he said, "since many are courageous but unjust, and there are those who are just, in turn, but not wise."

330a   "So then these too are parts of virtue," I said, "wisdom and courage?"

"Doubtless above all else," he said. "And wisdom is the *greatest* of the parts."

"And is each one of them distinct from the other?"

"Yes."

"And does each of them have a power[85] peculiar to it, just as with the parts of the face? An eye is not such as the ears, nor is its power the same; nor is any of the others such as another with respect to its power or in other ways. Is it the case then too that each of the parts
330b   of virtue is not such as another, either it itself or its power? Or is it indeed clear that this is so, if in fact it is comparable to the example at least?"

"But thus," he said, "it is, Socrates."

And I said, "None of the other parts of virtue, then, is such as knowledge; nor such as justice; nor such as courage; nor such as moderation; nor such as piety." He said no. "Come, then," I said, "let's examine in common what sort of thing each of them is, beginning with
330c   the following sort of thing: is justice a certain thing[86] or is it not a thing? For in my opinion it is; what's your opinion?"

"In mine too," he said.

"What then? If someone should ask me and you, 'Protagoras and Socrates, the two of you tell me, this thing that you two just now named, justice, is it itself just or unjust?' I would answer him that it is just, but what vote would you cast? The same as mine or different?"

"The same," he said.

"'Justice, then, is such a sort of thing as to be such as the just,' I for my part would say in answer to the questioner. Would you as well?"
330d   "Yes," he said.

---

85. Or, "capacity."
86. *Pragma*: that which is the object of action or concern, and even (as at 341d) that which causes one trouble; see also n. 5.

"If then after this he should ask us, 'Do you[87] assert then that piety too is something?' we would assert that it is, as I suppose."

"Yes," he said.

"'Would you assert, then, that this too is a certain thing?'[88] We would assert it, no?" He agreed to this too. "'Do you assert that this very thing is by nature of such a sort as to be such as the impious or such as the pious?' For my part," I said, "I would be indignant at the question and would say, 'Hush,[89] fellow! Nothing else would be pi-
330e ous, if piety itself will not be.' But what about you? Wouldn't you answer in this way?"

"Absolutely," he said.

"If then he should next say in his questioning of us, 'What then did you mean a little while ago? Did I not hear you correctly? For in my opinion you asserted that the parts of virtue are related to one another in such a way that one of them is not such as another.' For my part I would say, 'As regards the rest, you did hear correctly, but you misheard in that you think I too say this. It was Protagoras here who was
331a giving these answers, while I was doing the questioning.' If then he should say, 'Is what this fellow here says true, Protagoras? Do you assert that one part is not such as another of the parts of virtue? Is this your argument?' What would you answer him?"

"It would be necessary, Socrates," he said, "to agree."

"What then will we answer him, Protagoras, since we agree about this, if he asks us further: 'Piety, then, is not a thing such as the just, nor is justice such as the pious, but rather such as that which is not pious; and piety is such as that which is not just, but therefore unjust,
331b the just being impious?'[90] What will we answer him? For I myself, on my own behalf, would assert both that justice is pious and piety just. I would answer these same things on your behalf too, should you permit me to do so, because[91] either justice is the same thing as piety or it is as similar as possible, and above all else justice is such as piety and piety such as justice. Just see if you prevent me from giving this answer, or whether this is your opinion as well."

---

87. The plural "you," here and throughout this section.
88. *Pragma*: see n. 86.
89. Literally, "speak well" or "speak good omens." The verb (*euphemeō*) is often used when another has said something highly improper or even impious.
90. The reading of the principal mss. appears to be nonsensical ("And piety is such as that which is not just, but therefore just"), and the slight change needed to make sense of the phrase, which has in addition some ms. authority, is accepted by all modern editors.
91. Following the suggestion of Adam and Adam; "that" is another possible translation.

331c   "It's really not my opinion, Socrates," he said, "that it is so simple as for me to concede that justice is pious and piety just. In my opinion there is a distinction there. But what difference does this make?" he said. "If you like, let justice be for us pious and piety just."

   "That won't do for me," I said. "For I have no need to put to the test[92] this 'if you like' and 'if that's your opinion,' but rather me and you. And I say this 'me and you' because I think the argument would
331d   be best put to the test if one rids it of these 'if's.'"

   "Well," he said, "justice does resemble piety in some way. For anything whatever resembles anything else in some way or other: white resembles black in some way, and the hard the soft, and the other things that are held to be most contrary to one another. And the things that we previously asserted to have a different power and not to be such as one another—the parts of the face—they too resemble and are such as one another, at least in some way or other. So you might
331e   put these things too to the test in this way, if you like, on the grounds that *all* things are similar to one another. But it isn't just to call things having some similarity 'similar,' nor to call things having some dissimilarity 'dissimilar,' even if the similarity they have is very small."

   I was filled with wonder and said to him, "Are the just and the pious related to one another, according to you, such that they have only some small similarity to one another?"
332a   "Hardly so," he said, "but neither is it in turn as you, in my opinion, think it to be."

   "Well, now," I said, "since in my opinion you are finding this annoying, let's leave it be and instead make a thorough examination of this other point you were speaking of: do you call something 'foolishness'?"[93] He said that he did. "Isn't wisdom the complete contrary of this thing?"

   "In my opinion, at least," he said.

   "Whenever human beings act correctly and advantageously, are they then in your opinion being moderate in so acting, or if they were to act in the contrary manner?"[94]

   "They are being moderate," he said.
332b   "Are they moderate by means of moderation?"

---

92. Or, "refute."
93. *Aphrosunē*: the root of the word is related to that of the word translated as "moderation" (*sōphrosunē*: see n. 69), a relation Socrates will soon make use of.
94. The reading of the mss. The modern editors alter the text to read, in translation, "are they then in your opinion being moderate in so acting, or the contrary?"

"Necessarily."

"Are those who act incorrectly acting foolishly and, in so acting, not being moderate?"

"That's my opinion too," he said.

"Then is acting foolishly the contrary of acting moderately?" He said that that was so. "Are things done foolishly done by means of foolishness, things done moderately by means of moderation?" He agreed.

"If then something is done by means of strength, is it done in a strong way, and if something is done through weakness, in a weak way?" That was his opinion. "And if something is done with speed, 332c speedily, and if with slowness, slowly?" He said that that was so. "And if indeed something is done in a given manner, it is done through that same thing, and if in a contrary manner, through the contrary?" He agreed. "Come, then," I said, "is there something noble?" He conceded that there was. "Is there some contrary to this apart from the shameful?"

"There isn't."

"What then? Is there something good?"

"There is."

"Is there some contrary to this apart from the bad?"

"There isn't."

"What, then? Is there something that is high-pitched?" He said that there was. "Is there some other contrary to this apart from the low?" He said no. "Is there, then," I said, "for each one of the contraries, only one contrary and not many?" He agreed.

332d   "Come, then," I said, "let's sum up our agreements. Have we agreed that each thing has only one contrary, and not more?"

"We have agreed."

"And that that which is done in a contrary manner is done through the contraries?" He said that that was so. "And have we agreed that that which is done foolishly is done in a manner contrary to that which is done moderately?" He said that that was so. "And that that which is done moderately is done through moderation, that done 332e foolishly through foolishness?" He conceded this. "If in fact it is done in a contrary manner, then, would it be done through the contrary?"

"Yes."

"And the one thing is done through moderation, the other through foolishness?"

"Yes."

"In a contrary manner?"

"Certainly."

"Then would they be done through contrary things?"[95]

"Yes."

"Is foolishness the contrary of moderation?"

"It appears so."

"Do you[96] recall, then, that, in what came before, foolishness was agreed by us to be the contrary of wisdom?" He agreed. "And that one thing has only one contrary?"

"I assert that that's so."

333a "Which of the two arguments, Protagoras, are we to be rid of? The one according to which one thing has only one contrary, or that in which it was said that wisdom is different from moderation but each is a part of virtue and, in addition to its being different, they are dissimilar both in themselves and in regard to their powers, just like the parts of the face? So which one indeed are we to be rid of? For both of these arguments are not very musically stated: they don't sing the same tune or harmonize with one another. For how could they sing
333b the same tune, if in fact it's necessary that one thing have only one contrary and not more, on the one hand, and on the other that wisdom and moderation, in turn, appear to be contraries of foolishness, which is itself one? Is this the case, Protagoras," I said, "or is it otherwise?" He agreed, albeit very unwillingly. "Would moderation and wisdom, then, be one? And then justice and piety, in turn, became manifest to us previously as being pretty much the same thing.

"Come, now, Protagoras," I said, "let's not grow weary but instead make a thorough investigation of what remains as well. Is it your
333c opinion that some unjust person is moderate, because he commits injustice?"

"For my part, Socrates," he said, "I would be ashamed to agree to this, although many of the human beings do assert it."

"Shall I fashion my arguments with a view to them," I said, "or to you?"

"To begin with, if you like," he said, "conduct the conversation with a view to this argument of the many."

95. Literally, "beings" (*onta*).
96. The mss. read, "Do I recall . . . ?"

"Well, it makes no difference to me, provided you do answer, whether or not you give your own opinion. For it's the argument that I for my part am examining above all, although it turns out that I am equally examining both myself as questioner and the one answering."

333d   Now at first Protagoras was playing coy[97] with us—he criticized the argument for being annoying[98]—but subsequently he agreed to answer.

"Come, then," I said, "answer me from the beginning. Is it your opinion that some are being moderate by acting unjustly?"

"Let it be so," he said.

"And do you mean by 'being moderate,' being sensible?"[99] He said that he did. "And by 'being sensible,' deliberating well, because they are being unjust?"

"Let it be so," he said.

"If they fare well by being unjust," I said, "or if they fare badly?"

"If they fare well."

"Do you say, then, that some things are good?"

"I do say so."

"Well, then," I said, "are those things good that are advantageous to human beings?"

333e   "Yes, by Zeus!" he said, "and even if they aren't advantageous to human beings, I at least call them good!"

By this time Protagoras was in my opinion feeling riled up for a fight and contentious, and he stood prepared, as for battle, to answer me. So when I saw him in this state, I proceeded with caution and gently asked him, "Do you mean, Protagoras," I said, "things that are
334a   advantageous to no human being, or things that are not advantageous at all? Do you call even such sorts of things good?"

"Not at all," he said. "But for my part I know many things that are disadvantageous to human beings—food and drink and drugs and ten thousand others—but some that are advantageous. Some things are neither the one nor the other for human beings, but are for horses; some are only for cattle, others for dogs. And some things are for none of these but are for trees. And some things are good for the roots of

97. Translated as "to preen himself" in its only other appearance in the dialogue (317c). The root of the word suggests a desire to put on a false and flattering appearance.
98. Or, perhaps, "difficult" (see also 332a).
99. Literally, "thinking well" (*eu phronein*).

the tree but harmful to the young shoots. Manure, for example, dis-
334b tributed on the roots of all plants is good, but should you be willing
to put it on budding branches and young twigs, it destroys them all.
Olive oil too is quite bad for all plants and highly detrimental to the
hair of all the other animals apart from that of the human: to human
hair, and to the rest of the body, it is an aid to health.

"The good is something so complicated and varied that the same
334c thing that is good for things outside the human body is worst of all
for things within it. And for this reason all physicians forbid those in
a weakened condition from making use of olive oil, except in the
smallest amounts on what they are to eat, and then only enough to
prevent them from perceiving any annoying odors from their food
and relishes."

When he said these things, those present burst out in applause to
show that he'd spoken well, and I said: "Protagoras, I happen to be a
334d forgetful fellow, and if somebody speaks to me at length, I forget what
the speech is about. Now just as if I happened to be a little hard of
hearing, you'd think it necessary, if in fact you were going to converse
with me, to speak more loudly to me than to the others—so too now,
since you've met up with a forgetful person, cut short your answers
for me and make them briefer, if I'm to keep up with you."

"How then are you bidding me to answer briefly? Or am I to answer you," he said, "more briefly than is required?"

"Not at all," I said.

"But as much as is required?" he said.

334e "Yes," I said.

"Then am I to answer you so much as is required according to my
opinion, or according to yours?"

"Well, I've heard, at least," I said, "that you yourself are able—and
can teach another as well—to give answers about the same things
both at length if you want to, so that the argument never runs dry,
335a and so briefly, in turn, that nobody speaks more briefly than you. So
if you're going to converse with me, use this other way with me, that
of brief speeches."

"Socrates," he said, "by now I've entered into debates with many
human beings, and if I had done what you are bidding me to do—if
I had conversed with my opponent as he bade me to converse—I
never would have come to sight as better than anyone, nor would the
name 'Protagoras' have become known among the Greeks."

And I—for I knew that he himself was not satisfied with his own
335b previous answers and that he would not be willing of his own accord
to conduct the conversation by supplying answers—I came to the belief that it was no longer my task to remain at the get-together. I said,
"Well, you know, Protagoras, I'm not comfortable either with our get-
together coming to pass in a way contrary to what seems best to you.
But when you want to converse in a way that I'm capable of keeping
up with, then I'll converse with you. For even you yourself assert, as
is said about you, that you're able to conduct get-togethers with both
335c long and short speeches—for you are wise. But I'm incapable of these
long ones, though I'd like to be so able. You who are capable of both
ought to have yielded to us, so that the get-together might have come
to pass. But now I'm off, since you're unwilling and I have some business to attend to and wouldn't be able to stay while you draw out
your long speeches—there's somewhere I have to go—though I
might perhaps hear even these things not without pleasure." And as
I was saying this I began to get up as if to leave.

As I stood up, Callias held my hand in his right and got hold of my
335d simple cloak here with his left and said, "We won't let you go,
Socrates, for if you do leave, our conversations won't be the same. So
I ask you to stay with us; there's no one to whom I would listen with
greater pleasure than you and Protagoras in conversation. Just gratify us all in this."

By this time I was already standing as though to go, and I said, "Son
of Hipponicus, for my part I've always admired your love of wis-
335e dom,[100] but now I praise and love it. I'd want as a result to gratify
you, if you were to ask of me things I could do. But as things stand,
it is just as if you were to ask me to keep up with Crison[101] of Himera,
in his prime as a runner, or to run against and keep up with one of
the middle- or long-distance runners; I'd say to you that I ask it of
336a myself to follow these runners, much more than you do of me, but
I'm just unable to do it. Instead, if there's some need to watch me and
Crison running a race, ask him to make concessions to me: I'm unable to run quickly, but he can run slowly. So if you want to listen to
me and Protagoras, ask him to answer now just as he was answering

100. Literally, "philosophy."
101. A famous Olympic runner, mentioned in the *Laws* (840a) as being renowned for his
chastity during training.

me at first, briefly and with regard to the questions themselves. Oth-
336b erwise, what will be the manner of the conversation? For my part, I
supposed that getting together to converse with one another was different from making a public harangue."

"But you see, Socrates," he said, "Protagoras seems to speak justly
in claiming that it is his right to speak however he wants, and you in
turn in whatever way you want."

Then Alcibiades intervened and said, "What you say isn't noble,
Callias.[102] For Socrates here agrees that he has no share in Protagoras' lengthy speechmaking and yields to him in that. But that he is ca-
336c pable of conversing and knows how both to give and to receive an
account—I would marvel if he yields in these to any human being.
So if Protagoras agrees that he's paltrier than Socrates at conversing,
that's enough for Socrates. But if he resists this, let them converse by
means of question and answer, not by drawing out a long speech for
every question, evading the arguments and being unwilling to give
336d an account, going on at length until the many among the listeners forget what the question was about. For I guarantee Socrates won't forget anything—not but that he jokes and says he is forgetful. In my
opinion,[103] then, what Socrates says is more equitable—for each
must make manifest his own judgment."

After Alcibiades, I think it was Critias who spoke. "Prodicus and
Hippias, Callias is in my opinion very much on Protagoras' side, and
336e Alcibiades always loves to win in whatever it is he's after. But we
shouldn't side with either Socrates or Protagoras. We in common
should instead ask them both not to put an end to the get-together
halfway through."

337a When he'd said this, Prodicus said, "In my opinion what you say
is noble, Critias. For those present at speeches of this kind ought to
listen in common to both interlocutors, but not 'equally.' That is not
the same thing. For they should listen to both in common but not al-
lot equal weight to each; they should instead give more to the wiser,
less to the less learned. And I myself, Protagoras and Socrates, I think
it right for you to come to agreement and to dispute about the argu-
337b ments with one another but not to 'quarrel': it is with good will that

102. Alcibiades' remark contains an alliterative jingle: *kalōs . . . ō Kallia.*
103. Or, "It seems best to me that . . ." Here Alcibiades adopts the language of the resolu-
tions of the democratic assembly and urges those present to cast their own votes.

friends dispute with friends, but those who are at odds and are enemies quarrel with one another. And thus our get-together would
come to pass most beautifully. For in this way you the speakers
would be especially esteemed by us the listeners and not 'praised'—
for esteem stems from the souls of the listeners without deception,
but praise in argument is often given by those who speak falsely con-
337c   trary to their opinion. And we the listeners, in turn, would in this way
be especially delighted, not 'pleased'—for feeling delight belongs to
one who learns something and who shares in prudence[104] by means
of the intellect itself, whereas being pleased belongs to one who eats
something or who experiences another pleasure by means of the
body itself."

Very many of those present accepted what Prodicus said. After
Prodicus, Hippias the wise spoke. "You men who are present," he
said, "I hold that you are all kin and relatives and fellow citizens—
337d   by nature, not by law. For like is by nature akin to like, but law, being
a tyrant over human beings, compels many things through force, contrary to nature.[105] So I hold that it is shameful for us to know the nature of things—we who are wisest of the Greeks and who've come
together now for this very thing in the very hall of wisdom in
Greece,[106] and in this the greatest and most prosperous house in that
very city—and yet not to display for ourselves anything worthwhile
337e   of this worthy matter but to be at odds with one another like the paltriest of human beings.

"So I both ask and advise you, Protagoras and Socrates, to arrive
338a   at a common ground, using us as your arbiters. And you, don't seek
out that precise form[107] of the conversations that is excessively brief,
if that isn't pleasing to Protagoras, but let go and loosen the reins of
the speeches so they may appear to us more magnificent and attractive. Protagoras, in turn, don't let all the sails unfurl, propelled by a
favorable wind, and seek refuge on an open sea of speeches so that
land is lost sight of. Instead, both of you keep to a middle course. So
do this, and be persuaded by me to elect an arbitrator and overseer

104. *Phronēsis*, the first appearance in the dialogue of this term.
105. Hippias here refers to the common proverb that like is attracted to like (see, e.g.,
Homer, *Odyssey* 17.218) and perhaps to Pindar's verse concerning the rule of law (see *Gorgias* 484b).
106. That is, Athens.
107. *Eidos*, one of the terms Socrates uses in his so-called theory of Forms or Ideas.

and prytanis who will watch out for us that the length of the speeches
338b of each be measured."

These things were pleasing to those present,[108] and all offered their
praise. Callias said that he wouldn't let me go, and they asked me to
elect an overseer. So I said that it would be shameful to elect an um-
pire of the speeches. "For either the one elected will be inferior to us,
in which case it wouldn't be correct for the inferior to oversee the
better; or he will be similar and this wouldn't be correct either: one
who is similar to us will also do similar things so that his election
338c will have been superfluous. So you'll elect one who is better than we
are instead. In truth it's impossible, as I think, for you to elect someone wiser than Protagoras here. And if you'll elect one who is no better but merely assert that he is, then this too becomes a point of
shame for Protagoras here, to elect an overseer as if he were a paltry
fellow.

"As for what concerns me, it makes no difference to me. But I am
willing to do the following so that what you're eager about, our get-
338d together and conversation, may come to pass: if Protagoras doesn't
want to answer, let him ask. I'll do the answering and at the same time
try to show him how I say one answering ought to do so. And when
I've answered as much as he wants to ask, then let him once again
render an account to me in similar fashion. If he doesn't seem eager
to answer by sticking to the question itself, you and I in common will
ask him what in fact you are asking of me, not to ruin the get-together.
338e And for this there is no need to have a single overseer, but you all will
oversee things in common." Everyone was of the opinion that this
was what ought to be done. And Protagoras was very unwilling, but
nonetheless he was compelled to agree to ask and, when he'd asked
sufficiently, to give an account again by answering briefly. So he began to ask in about the following way.

"I believe, Socrates," he said, "that the greatest part of a man's education is to be terrific at what pertains to verses. This means to be
339a able to understand which of the things said by the poets have been
correctly written and which not, and to know how to analyze them
and give an account when questioned. And for now in particular, the

---

108. Or, perhaps, "These things were resolved upon by those present." The language
Socrates here uses can refer to the resolution of a deliberative body and so reinforces the
suggestion that their group forms some such body.

question will concern the same thing that you and I are now conversing[109] about, namely virtue, but transferred into the realm of poetry. That will be the only difference.

"For Simonides[110] says somewhere to Scopas, the son of Creon of Thessaly,[111] that

339b   Now[112] a good man truly it is difficult to become,
       In hands and feet and mind four-square, forged without blame.

"Do you know this ode, or am I to go through it all for you?"

And I said, "There's no need, for I know it, and in fact I happen to have devoted considerable attention to the lyric."

"Good," he said. "So is it your opinion that it has been beautifully[113] and correctly written or not?

"Very correctly," I for my part said.[114]

"And is it your opinion that it has been beautifully written, if the poet contradicts himself?"

"It wouldn't be beautifully written," I said.

"Take a better look at it," he said.

339c   "But, good one, I have examined it adequately."

"Then you know," he said, "that he says later on in the lyric,

       And the saying of Pittacus[115] does not seem to me to be fitting,
       Though uttered by a wise mortal; it is difficult, says he, to be noble.[116]

"Are you considering that this same person says both these and the previous things?"

"I know it," I said.

"Is it your opinion then," he said, "that the latter are consistent with the former?"

---

109. Croiset, following one ms., reads: "the same thing that you and I were just now conversing about."

110. A famous poet from Ceos (circa 556–468 B.C.). The interpretation of one of his verses figures prominently in book 1 of the *Republic*.

111. The Scopadae were a ruling clan in parts of Thessaly, in praise of whom Simonides composed several poems.

112. Or, "on the one hand": the line contains a common asseverative or antithetical particle (*men*) that does not admit of a single translation.

113. Or, "nobly."

114. The reading of two mss. The modern editors follow Bekker in adding the adverb "beautifully" ("nobly") to Socrates' reply, but it is not present in the Greek.

115. Pittacus (circa 650–570 B.C.) was ruler of Mytilene and was regarded as a wise man.

116. Not the word elsewhere translated as "noble" (*kalos*) but the more poetic *esthlos*, which in general denotes a thing good of its kind and, when applied to human beings, may mean morally good, brave, or stout. The two words may be simply equivalent here, but the appearance of *esthlos* will be noted.

"They appear to be, at least to me"—though at the same time I was afraid that he was making sense. "But," I said, "don't they appear to you to be?"

339d   "How could one who says both of these things appear to be consistent—he who at first supposed that 'it is difficult to become a good man in truth,' but forgot it a little later on in the poem and criticizes Pittacus for saying the same things that he himself says—'it is difficult to be noble'[117]—and refuses to accept it when Pittacus says the same things as he himself does? And yet whenever he criticizes one who says the same things as he himself does, it's clear that he criticizes himself as well, so that, either in what came before or in what came later, he doesn't speak correctly."

When he'd said these things, many of his listeners voiced their tumultuous approval. And at first, just as if I'd been struck by a good
339e   boxer, I was made dizzy and woozy by what he'd said and by the uproar of the others. Then—so that I'd have time to consider what the poet meant, to tell you the truth—I turned to Prodicus and called to him. "Prodicus," I said, "Simonides is of course your fellow citi-
340a   zen.[118] It's your just duty to come to the man's aid, so I think I'll summon you. Just as Homer said that Scamander, being besieged by Achilles, summoned Simois, saying,

Dear brother, let us both check the mighty strength of the man[119]

so I too summon you, lest Protagoras sack our Simonides. For the restoration[120] of Simonides also requires your musical[121] skill by means of which you distinguish 'wanting' from 'desiring' as not be-
340b   ing the same thing, and the many noble things you said just now. So now consider if you share my opinion, for Simonides doesn't appear to contradict himself. Prodicus, you declare your judgment: is 'to become' the same thing as 'to be' in your opinion, or different?"

"Different, by Zeus!" Prodicus said.

"Didn't Simonides himself declare his own judgment in the first lines," I said, "that it is in truth difficult to become a good man?"
340c   "What you say is true," Prodicus said.

---

117. *Esthlos.*
118. Both hailed from Iulis on the island of Ceos.
119. Homer, *Iliad* 21.308–09.
120. Or, "correction."
121. That is, a skill pertaining to the Muses, a signification that includes, but is also much broader than, what we mean by "music."

"And he criticizes Pittacus," I said, "not, as Protagoras supposes, because he says the same thing as himself, but something different. For Pittacus didn't say that it is difficult *to become* noble,[122] as did Simonides, but *to be* such. And, Protagoras, 'to be' is not the same thing as 'to become,' as Prodicus here affirms. But if 'to be' is not the same thing as 'to become,' then Simonides doesn't contradict himself. And

340d perhaps Prodicus here and many others would say, with Hesiod, that to become good is difficult—for

before virtue the gods placed sweat

but whenever someone

reaches the apex of it, then it is easy to possess, difficult though it was.[123]

When Prodicus heard this, he praised me. But Protagoras said, "Your correction,[124] Socrates, contains a greater error than the one you would correct."

And I said, "Then I've done my work badly, as it seems, Protago-

340e ras, and I'm a sort of laughable physician: in applying my treatment I make the illness worse."

"But so it is," he said.

"How's that?" I said.

"It would be great ignorance on the part of the poet," he said, "if he asserts that virtue is something so paltry to possess, when it is the most difficult thing of all, as is the opinion of all human beings."

And I said, "By Zeus, Prodicus here has happened to be present at our speeches at just the right time. For you see it's likely, Protagoras,

341a that Prodicus' is a certain divine wisdom of long ago, which either began in the time of Simonides or else is even more ancient still. And although you are experienced in many other things, you appear to be inexperienced in it—unlike me, for I'm experienced on account of being the student of Prodicus here.

"And now, in my opinion, you don't understand that perhaps Simonides was not taking this word 'difficult' as you are taking it, but just as Prodicus here always admonishes me about the word 'terrible' whenever I praise either you or someone else by saying that Pro-

341b tagoras is a terribly wise man, he asks me if I'm not ashamed to call

122. *Esthlos.*
123. See Hesiod, *Works and Days* 289–92. Hesiod's text as it has come down to us differs slightly from Socrates' quote or paraphrase of it.
124. The same word translated as "restoration" (see n. 120).

the good things terrible—for the terrible, he asserts, is bad. At any rate, nobody ever says 'terrible wealth' or 'terrible peace' or 'terrible health' but rather 'terrible illness' and 'terrible war' and 'terrible poverty,' on the grounds that the terrible is bad. So perhaps the Ceans and Simonides take the word 'difficult,' in turn, either as being bad or as something else you don't understand.

"So let's ask Prodicus—it's just to ask him about Simonides' di-

341c   alect. What did Simonides mean by 'difficult,' Prodicus?"

"'Bad,'" he said.

"So for these reasons, Prodicus," I said, "he also criticizes Pittacus for saying that 'it's difficult to be noble,'[125] just as if he heard him say, 'It's bad to be noble.'"[126]

"But what do you think Simonides means, Socrates," he said, "other than this? Wasn't he reproaching Pittacus because he didn't know how to distinguish the words correctly, being from Lesbos and having been raised with a barbarian dialect?"

"So do you hear Prodicus here, Protagoras?" I said. "Do you have

341d   anything to say in opposition to this?"

And Protagoras said, "It's far from being this way, Prodicus. But I know well that Simonides too meant what the rest of us mean by 'difficult'—not 'bad' but what isn't easy and comes into being with many troubles."[127]

"But I too, Protagoras, think that Simonides means this," I said, "and that Prodicus here knows it as well but is joking and thinks it fitting to test you to see if you can come to the aid of your own argument. For that Simonides doesn't mean 'bad' by the word 'difficult,'

341e   there is a great proof in the immediately following line. For he says that,

>   god alone could have this prize

Doubtless he doesn't say this, that it's bad 'to be noble,'[128] then assert that the god alone could have this and assign this prize to the god alone. For Prodicus would be saying that Simonides is some sort of a licentious person and in no way a Cean.[129] But I'm willing to tell you

125. *Esthlos.*
126. *Esthlos.*
127. *Pragmata,* the plural of *pragma*: see nn. 5 and 86.
128. *Esthlos.*
129. The Ceans had the reputation of being an upright people: see, e.g., *Laws* 638b and Aristophanes, *Frogs* 970.

what in my opinion Simonides has in mind in this lyric, if you want
342a   to test me as to where I stand concerning verses,[130] as you put it. But
if you want, I'll listen to you."

When Protagoras heard me say this, he said, "If that's what you
want, Socrates." But both Prodicus and Hippias strongly bade me to
do so, as did the others.

"Well," I said, "I'll try to go through for you[131] my opinions, at least,
concerning this lyric. Now philosophy is most ancient and most abun-
342b   dant among the Greeks in both Crete and Lacedaemon,[132] and the
most abundant number of sophists on earth are there. But they utterly
deny this and pretend to be without learning so that it won't be
patently obvious that they owe their supremacy among the Greeks to
wisdom—like those who Protagoras was saying are the sophists—
and so they may be held to owe their supremacy to fighting and
courage. They believe that, if it were known what constituted their supremacy, namely wisdom, all would practice it. But as things stand,
they've concealed this and have thoroughly deceived the Laconizers
in the cities, those who, by imitating the Lacedaemonians, have cau-
342c   liflower ears and wear boxing gloves and love physical training and
wear short cloaks, on the grounds that it is indeed through these
things that the Lacedaemonians hold sway over the Greeks.

"But the Lacedaemonians, whenever they want to get together
freely with the sophists among them and are vexed by their clandes-
tine meetings, they issue an expulsion order[133] against both these Laconizers and any other foreigner who may be visiting, and they get
together with the sophists unbeknownst to the foreigners.
342d   "And like the Cretans, they don't permit any of the young to go out
to other cities so that the young won't unlearn what they themselves
teach them. And it is not only men in these cities who pride themselves

130. Socrates here uses the same word (*epōn*) that Protagoras had used at the opening of his
remarks on poetry (338e).
131. The plural "you."
132. Another name for Sparta. As two commentators put it, the Spartans "were not philosophers but a notoriously dour and uncultivated people of few words and fewer ideas. They
lived in a state of perpetual military readiness, and brought up their young under a brutally
tough regimen" (B. A. F. Hubbard and E. S. Karnofsky, *Plato's Protagoras* [Chicago: University of Chicago Press, 1982], 129–30). See in general Xenophon, *Constitution of the Lacedaemonians*, and Aristotle, *Politics* 2.9.
133. On the Spartan practice of expelling foreigners, see, e.g., Thucydides 1.144; Aristophanes, *Birds* 1012–13; Xenophon, *Constitution of the Lacedaemonians* 14.4; Plutarch, *Lycur-
gus* 27.

on education, but women too.[134] You would know that what I say is true and that the Lacedaemonians have been best educated with a view to philosophy and speeches,[135] by the following: if someone is willing to get together with the paltriest of Lacedaemonians, he will discover that, for the most part, the Lacedaemonian does indeed ap-

342e pear to be a paltry fellow when it comes to speeches. But then, at a certain point in what's being said, he throws out a brief and pithy utterance, one worthy of account, just like a terrific javelin thrower, with the result that his interlocutor appears no better than a child. Some of those nowadays and some of the ancients have grasped well this very thing, that to Laconize is much more to love wisdom[136] than it is to love physical training, for they know that such sayings can be uttered

343a only by a perfectly educated human being. Among these were Thales the Milesian, Pittacus the Mytilenaean, Bias the Prienean, our own Solon, Cleoboulus the Lindian, Myson the Chenaean, and the seventh among these was said to be a Lacedaemonian, Chilon.[137] All these were emulators and erotic lovers and students of the Lacedaemonians' education, and one could learn that their wisdom was of this sort from the brief and lapidary sayings that each stated; and when they came together in common as well they offered up the first fruits of wis-

343b dom to Apollo at the temple in Delphi, where they wrote the things that indeed all recite, 'Know Thyself' and 'Nothing in Excess.'

"Why then do I say this? Because this was the character of the philosophy of the ancients, namely a certain Laconic brevity of speech. And in particular this saying of Pittacus was circulated in private and praised by the wise, 'To be noble[138] is difficult.'

343c "So Simonides, because he was ambitious[139] when it came to wisdom, realized that if he should bring down this saying and prevail over it, just as if it were a highly regarded athlete, then he himself would be highly regarded by the human beings of that time. It was against this saying, then, and for the sake of this end, that he wrote the entire lyric, plotting to discredit it, as it appears to me.

"So let's all in common make a thorough investigation as to

---

134. On the education of the Spartan women, see Aristotle, *Politics* 1269b12–1270a11.
135. *Logoi.*
136. Or, "to philosophize."
137. The traditional list of the seven wise men varies somewhat, Periander of Corinth and Epimenides of Crete appearing in some versions (see, e.g., Diogenes Laertius 1.22–122).
138. *Esthlos.*
139. Literally, a "lover of honor" (*philotimos*).

whether what I say is true. For right away the first part of the lyric would appear mad if, in wanting to say that it is difficult to become 343d a good man, he then inserted the 'now.'[140] For this appears to have been inserted without any reason—unless one supposes that Simonides here speaks as if he is quarreling with the saying of Pittacus. When Pittacus says that 'it is difficult to be noble,'[141] Simonides disputes this and says, 'No, but now to become a good man is difficult, Pittacus, truly.' Not truly *good*—he doesn't mean the 'truly' to apply to this—as though there are some who are truly good and others who 343e are good but not truly so. For that, at any rate, would appear to be naïve and not characteristic of Simonides. Instead, one must posit the 'truly' as a hyperbaton[142] in the lyric, thus taking the saying of Pittacus as a kind of preface, as though we were to have Pittacus himself speaking and Simonides giving his reply: 'O Human Beings, it is dif-344a ficult to be noble,'[143] and Simonides answers, 'Pittacus, what you say isn't true. For not *to be* but now[144] *to become* a good man, in hands and feet and mind four-square, forged without blame, is truly difficult.' Thus it appears reasonable that the 'now' was inserted and that the 'truly' is correctly placed at the end. And all that comes later bears witness to this, that this is what was meant. For there are many things 344b pertaining to each of the sayings in the lyric that show that it was well written—it is very gracefully and carefully done—but it would be a great task to go through it in this way. Instead, let's go through carefully its general outline and intention, namely that there assuredly is a refutation of Pittacus' saying throughout the lyric.

"For he next says, a little later on (if we put it as though he were giving an argument in prose),[145] that now to become a good man is truly difficult, and yet it is possible for a certain time, at least; but for one who has become such to remain in that state and to be a good 344c man—what you are saying, Pittacus—is impossible and not human, but god alone would have this prize:

---

140. The same asseverative particle as indicated in n. 112.
141. *Esthlos.*
142. The first recorded instance of this grammatical term meaning the separation of words or phrases naturally belonging together. Socrates' point is that Simonides meant for the adverbial "truly" or "in truth" (*alatheōs* or *alētheiai*) to modify "difficult," not "good."
143. *Esthlos.*
144. Or, "rather": see nn. 112 and 140.
145. A *logos.*

but for a man it is not possible not to be bad,
Whom unmanageable misfortune brings down.

So whom does unmanageable misfortune bring down when it comes to the rule of a ship? Clearly not the unskilled layman, for the unskilled layman has always been down. Just as somebody couldn't lay low one who is lying down, but one could lay low somebody who was at some point standing so as to make him lie down, and not one already lying down, so also unmanageable misfortune could bring down one who 344d was once well able to manage but not one who is always unable to manage. A great storm that befalls a ship's pilot could make him unable to manage, and a harsh season that comes upon a farmer could render him unable to manage, and these same things apply to a physician.

"For it's possible for someone noble[146] to become bad, as is testified to by another poet, when he says:

But a good man is at one time bad, at another noble.[147]

But it isn't possible for the bad man to become—rather, he must nec-
344e essarily always be—such. As a result, whenever an unmanageable misfortune brings down one who is able to manage and is wise and good, 'it is not possible not to be bad.' But you assert, Pittacus, that 'it is difficult to be noble.'[148] In fact, becoming noble[149] is difficult yet possible, but to be it impossible.

For every man who has acted well[150] is good
But bad if badly.

345a "What then is good action when it comes to letters, and what makes a man good at letters? It's clear that it is the learning of these things. And what goodness of action makes a physician good? It's clear that it is learning how to tend to the sick. 'But bad, badly.' Who then could become a bad physician? It's clear that it would be one who is in the first place a physician, then a good physician—for he is the one who could also become bad. But we who are unskilled laymen in medicine could never become physicians or builders or any other such 345b thing by acting badly. And whoever could not become a physician by acting badly is clearly not a bad physician either.

"So also the good man could at one time become bad either

---

146. *Esthlos.*
147. *Esthlos*; Xenophon quotes the same line at *Memorabilia* 1.2.20.
148. *Esthlos.*
149. *Esthlos.*
150. Or, "fared well."

through the passage of time, or through toil or illness or some other calamity, for this alone constitutes bad action, namely being deprived of knowledge; but the bad man could never become bad—for he always is such—but if he is going to become bad, he must first become good. As a result, this part of the lyric too points in this direction, that

345c   on the one hand it is impossible to be a good man, as one who is good to the very end, but that on the other hand it is possible to become good and for this same man to become bad. And best for the longest time are those whom the gods love.[151]

"So all these things too were said against Pittacus, and the next parts of the lyric make this clearer still. For he says,

> For this reason I shall never set on a vain hope the meager span of life
> allotted, seeking that which cannot come to be:
> A human being wholly without blemish, among us who reap the fruit
> of the broad land.
> When I find him I shall tell you.

345d   So he says. Thus he zealously attacks the saying of Pittacus throughout the whole lyric.

> And I praise and love all
> Willingly whoever does
> Nothing shameful; but with necessity not even gods do battle.

This too was said with a view to the same point.

"For Simonides was not so uneducated as to say that he praises these—he who willingly does nothing bad—as though there are some who willingly do bad things. For I pretty much think that none of the

345e   wise men holds that any human being willingly errs or willingly carries out any shameful and bad deeds. Rather, they well know that all those who do the shameful and bad things do them unwillingly.

"And Simonides in particular doesn't assert that he is a praiser of these—he who doesn't do bad things willingly—but he says this 'willingly' in regard to himself. That is, he believed that a noble and good man[152] often compels himself to become the friend and praiser

346a   of someone, to love and praise him[153]—as often happens when, for example, a man is alienated from his mother or father or fatherland

---

151. I follow the suggested translation of Adam and Adam. Also possible is: "And [Also] best are those whom the gods love for the longest time." The phrase "for the longest time" (*epi pleiston*) may also mean "to the greatest extent."

152. Or, "gentleman": see n. 33.

153. The phrase "to love and praise him" is deleted by modern editors but is in the mss.

or any other such thing. He believed that whenever some such thing happens to the wicked, it is as if they take delight in seeing this and make a show of their blame, reproaching the wickedness of their parents or fatherland so that people won't accuse them of neglecting them or criticize them because they do neglect them. As a result, they blame them still more and heap willful enmities on top of those that
346b arise from compulsion.[154] But he believed that the good, by contrast, conceal all this and compel themselves to praise them; and if they are angered in some way by the injustice they suffer at the hands of their parents or fatherland, they talk themselves out of it and are reconciled, further compelling themselves to love their own and to praise them. And often, I think, Simonides too believed that he praised and wrote encomia for a tyrant or someone else of this sort, not willingly, but under self-compulsion.

"These things as well he says to Pittacus: 'Pittacus, it is not for this
346c reason that I blame you, because I am fond of blame, since—

For me at least it is enough, if one isn't bad
Nor overly reckless;[155] one who knows justice as benefactor of the city,
a sound man;
Him I will not blame.
For I am not fond of criticism:
Infinite are the generations of the fools.'

As a result, if someone delights in uttering reproaches, he could get his fill of it by blaming them.

All things, you see, are beautiful, with which shameful things have not been mixed
346d "In saying this it is not as if he were saying that all things, you see, are white, with which black has not been mixed—that would be laughable in several ways—but that he himself accepts the middling things in order not to utter blame. 'And I don't seek,' he said, ' "a human being wholly without blame / among us who reap the fruit of the broad land, / But when I find him I shall tell you . . . " ' As a result, I'll not praise anybody, with *this* as the standard; but for me it is enough if one is of a middling sort and does nothing bad, as "I love and praise all" '—and here he has used the dialect of the Mytile-

---

154. Or, "necessity." Reading Heusde's slight emendation, with the modern editors. The reading of the mss. translates as: "on top of the necessities."
155. The word (*apalamnos*) can also mean "helpless."

346e   naeans[156] because he is addressing the 'I praise and love all willingly'
to Pittacus. And it's necessary to punctuate here after the 'willingly':
'"I praise and love all willingly, whoever does nothing shameful,"
though there are some whom I praise and love unwillingly. So you,
even if you had said what is equitable and truthful in only a middling
347a   way, Pittacus, I never would have blamed you. But as it is, opinion
has it that you speak truthfully, but you are stating utter falsehoods[157]
about the greatest things, and for these reasons I do blame you.' In
my opinion, Prodicus and Protagoras," I said, "these were the things
Simonides had in mind in writing this lyric."

And Hippias said, "In my opinion, Socrates, you've gone through
347b   the lyric well. Yet I too," he said, "have an account of it that is good,
which I'll display to you[158] if you want."

And Alcibiades said, "Yes, Hippias, but another time. For now,
what Protagoras and Socrates each agreed to has the just claim—if
Protagoras still wants to ask, then Socrates answers, but if he wants
to answer Socrates, then Socrates asks."

And I said, "For my part I leave it to Protagoras, whichever of the
two is more pleasing to him. But if he wants to, let's leave be what
pertains to lyrics and poems. As for what concerns the points I asked
347c   you about to begin with, Protagoras, these I'd gladly bring to a conclusion by investigating them together with you. For in my opinion
conversing about poetry is most like the drinking parties of paltry
and common human beings: because they are incapable of getting together with one another just by themselves over drinks with their
own voices and their own speeches, on account of their lack of edu-
347d   cation, these people run up the price of aulos-girls, pay a great deal
for the foreign voice of the aulos, and conduct their get-togethers
with one another by listening to its voice.

"But wherever fellow drinkers are noble and good[159] and have
been educated, you wouldn't see aulos-girls or dancing girls or harp-
girls. Rather, it's enough for them to get together by themselves without such trifling and childish things and with the sound of just their

---

156. Socrates (or Simonides) uses the Aeolic form of the verb "to praise" (*epainumi* rather
than *epaineō*).
157. Or, "lies."
158. The plural "you."
159. Or, "gentlemen": see n. 33.

own voices, each of them speaking and listening in turn in an orderly
347e fashion, even if they drink a great deal of wine. So too such sorts of
get-togethers, if they take place with men of the kind many among
us assert we are, require neither a foreign sound nor poets, who cannot be asked what it is they are saying. These the many cite in their
speeches, some asserting that the poet thinks one thing, others something else, in this way conducting a conversation about something
they are unable to put to the test. But they[160] bid farewell to drinking
348a parties of this sort and get together with one another by themselves,
testing each other in the course of their own speeches by receiving
and giving such speeches.

"In my opinion, you and I ought rather to imitate men of this kind
and set aside the poets themselves in order to fashion speeches with
one another by ourselves, in this way making a test of the truth and
one another. And if you still want to ask questions, I'm prepared to
make myself available to you to answer. But if you want, make yourself available to me, so that we can go through the things we stopped
in the middle of and bring them to a conclusion."

348b   When I said this and other such things, Protagoras did not make at
all clear which of the two he would do. Then Alcibiades spoke, looking toward Callias: "Callias," he said, "is it your opinion that what
Protagoras is doing now is noble as well, when he's unwilling either
to give an account or to make clear that he won't? In my opinion, it
isn't. But either let him carry on a conversation or let him say that he
is unwilling to converse, so that we may know this of him and so that
Socrates may converse with somebody else, or whoever else wants to
may do so with another."

348c   Protagoras was ashamed, in my opinion at least, because of what
Alcibiades was saying and what Callias and almost all the others
present were asking for; and so he brought himself with difficulty to
continue the conversation and bade me to ask him questions so that
he might answer.

I said, "Protagoras, don't suppose that I am conversing with you
because I want anything other than to investigate thoroughly the
things that I myself am continually perplexed by. For I believe there
to be something considerable to what Homer says:

---

160. Presumably either the "educated fellow drinkers" mentioned at 347d or "the kind of
men many among us assert we are," if these are not one and the same.

348d   Two going together, and the one observed before the other[161]

for in this way, I suppose, all of us human beings have greater re-
sources with a view to every deed and speech and thought. 'But if
one alone observes,' then he immediately goes around seeking out
someone, until he happens upon him, to whom he may point this out
and with whom he may make certain of it. So for the sake of this I too
gladly converse with you more than with anyone else, believing you
to be best at investigating (in addition to other things) what it is rea-
348e   sonable for a decent man to investigate, and virtue in particular. For
who else other than you? It is not only that you suppose yourself to
be noble and good;[162] certain others are themselves decent but unable to make others such. But you both are good yourself and can
make others good, and you have had such faith in yourself that while
349a   others hide this art, you have had yourself openly heralded among
all the Greeks, have called yourself a sophist, and made yourself
known as a teacher of education and virtue, the first to think himself
deserving of pay for this. How then could I not summon you to the
inquiry into these things and ask you questions and consort with
you? It couldn't be otherwise.

"And now, as for the things I was asking about to begin with, my
desire is to have you remind me of some of them again from the beginning and for us together to make a thorough investigation of oth-
349b   ers of them. The question was, I think, the following: 'wisdom' and
'moderation' and 'courage' and 'justice' and 'piety'—do these things,
though they are five names, pertain to one thing, or does some particular being and thing underlie each of these names, each having its
own power, no one of them being such as another?

"You said that the names do not pertain to one thing but that each
349c   of these names attaches to a particular thing, that all of these are parts
of virtue, not as parts of gold are similar to one another and to the
whole of which they are parts but as the parts of the face are dissimilar to one another and to the whole of which they are parts, each having its particular power. If in your opinion these things still are as
before, say so. But if they are somehow different, specify this, for I at
least won't hold it against you at all if you now speak in a different

---

161. See Homer, *Iliad* 10.224 and following.
162. Or, "a gentleman": see n. 33.

way. For I wouldn't wonder if you were saying those things then just
349d   to test me."

"Well, I say to you, Socrates," he said, "that all these are parts of
virtue and that four of them are reasonably comparable to one another,
but courage is very different from them all. You'll know that what I say
is true from the following: you'll discover many human beings who are
very unjust and very impious and very licentious and very unlearned
but who are very courageous to a distinguished degree."

349e   "Now hold on," I said. "What you're saying is indeed worth investigating. Do you say that the courageous are bold,[163] or something
else?"

"They're even eager," he said, "in the face of things the many fear
to advance toward."[164]

"Come, then, do you assert virtue to be something noble, and is it
on the grounds that it is noble that you present yourself as a teacher
of it?"

"A most noble thing," he said, "unless I'm mad, that is!"

"So is some part of it shameful, another noble," I said, "or is the
whole of it noble?"

"The whole, surely, is as noble as anything can be."

350a   "Do you know, then, who dive boldly into wells?"

"I do indeed: the divers."

"Because they have knowledge, or on account of something else?"

"Because they have knowledge."

"And who are bold when it comes to waging war on horseback, the
skilled cavalry men or the unskilled ones?"

"The skilled cavalry men."

"And who when holding light shields? The skilled light-shieldsmen[165] or the unskilled ones?"

"The skilled light-shieldsmen. And as for all the other cases, if this
is what you are seeking," he said, "the knowers are bolder than the
non-knowers, and they themselves are more so once they've learned
350b   something than prior to it."

163. Or, "confident," "daring."
164. The adjective Protagoras here uses to describe the courageous is linked with the verb
"to go": the courageous are eager (*itas*) "to go" (*ienai*) against or toward things that frighten
the many.
165. Or, "peltasts."

"By now you've seen some," I said, "who, though they're without knowledge of any of these things, are bold in regard to each of them?"

"For my part," he said, "I have, and they're *overly* bold."

"So then are these bold ones courageous as well?"

"But in that case," he said, "courage would be a shameful thing: they are madmen!"

"How then," I said, "do you mean 'the courageous'? Didn't you say they're the bold?"

"I say that now as well," he said.

350c   "Then are these," I said, "who are bold in this way not courageous but manifestly mad? And then again those wisest ones are also boldest, and, being boldest, most courageous? And according to this account, wisdom would be courage?"

"You aren't making a noble recollection, Socrates," he said, "of what I was saying in response to you. For my part, when I was asked by you if the courageous are bold, I agreed. But I wasn't asked if the bold too are courageous—for if you had asked me then, I would have

350d   said that not all are. And as for the courageous not being bold, you've nowhere demonstrated that I was incorrect when I agreed [that they are bold]. Next you establish that the knowers are bolder than they themselves or others would be without knowledge, and on this basis you suppose that courage and wisdom are the same thing.

"Proceeding in this manner, you might suppose that strength too is wisdom. For, to begin with, if you should ask me, proceeding in this way, if the strong are powerful,[166] I would assert that they are.

350e   Next, if those who possess knowledge of wrestling are more powerful than those who do not possess knowledge of wrestling and are themselves more powerful once they've learned about it than they were before learning about it, I would assert that that is so. Once I had agreed to these things, it would be permissible for you to say, making use of these same pieces of evidence, that wisdom is strength according to what I'd agreed to. But I do not agree, here or elsewhere, that the powerful are strong, although the strong are powerful. For I

351a   don't agree that power and strength are the same thing. Instead, the one—power—comes into being from knowledge, as well as from craziness and spirited anger, the other—strength—from the nature and proper nurturing of bodies. So here again I don't agree that bold-

166. Or, "capable."

ness is the same thing as courage. It turns out as a result that the courageous are bold but not all the bold are courageous. For people come to possess boldness from art[167] as well as from spirited anger
351b   and craziness, just as in the case of power, but courage comes into being from the nature and proper nurturing of souls."

"Do you say, Protagoras," I said, "that some human beings live well, others badly?" He said that he did. "Is it your opinion then that a human being would live well if he should live with distress and pain?" He said no. "And what if he should come to the end having lived out his life pleasantly? Isn't it your opinion that he would have thus lived well?"

"That is my opinion, at any rate," he said.
351c   "Living pleasantly, then, is good, unpleasantly bad."

"If, that is, he should live his life by taking pleasure in the *noble* things," he said.

"What's this, Protagoras? Surely you too don't call some pleasant things bad and some distressing things good, as do the many? I mean, in that respect in which things are pleasant, aren't they good, unless something else arises from them? And again aren't the distressing things, insofar as they are distressing, similarly bad?"
351d   "I don't know, Socrates," he said, "if I ought to answer so simply, as the question you pose suggests, that *all* the pleasant things are good and the distressing things bad. Rather, in my opinion it's safer for me to reply not only with a view to the present answer but also with a view to the rest of my life as a whole: there are some pleasant things that aren't good, and there are in turn also some distressing things that aren't bad but some that are; and, third, there are some that are neither, neither bad nor good."

"Don't you call pleasant," I said, "the things that share in pleasure
351e   or produce pleasure?"

"Certainly," he said.

"Well, this is what I mean: insofar as things are pleasant, aren't they good? I'm asking whether the pleasure itself isn't good."

"Just as you always say, Socrates," he said, "let's examine it, and if the inquiry seems to be reasonable and the same thing appears to be both pleasant and good, we'll agree to it. But if not, then at that point we'll dispute it."

---

167. *Technē*: see n. 44.

"Do you want to lead the inquiry," I said, "or am I to lead it?"

"It's just for you to lead it," he said, "for you are also the one initiating the argument."

352a   "Might it become clear to us, then," I said, "in the following way? Just as if someone should say, when inquiring on the basis of one's outward appearance[168] either with a view to health or one of the body's tasks, and when looking at the face and hands: 'Come, now, uncover your chest and back and show them to me, so that I may make a more thorough examination,' so I too desire something like this for the inquiry. Having observed that you stand in regard to the good and the pleasant as you contend, I must say something like this: 'Come, now, Protagoras, uncover for me this aspect of your thought
352b   as well: how do you stand in regard to knowledge? Is your opinion about this too like that of the many human beings, or different? The opinion of the many concerning knowledge is something like this, that it isn't a strong thing characterized by either leadership or rule. They don't think about it as though it were any such thing at all, but often when knowledge is present in a human being, they think that it is not the knowledge that rules him but something else—now spirited anger, now pleasure, now pain, sometimes erotic love, many times fear. They simply think about knowledge as they do about a
352c   slave, that it is dragged around by all else.' So is your opinion about it something like this as well, or is it that knowledge is both noble and capable of ruling a human being, and that if in fact someone knows the good things and the bad, he won't be overpowered by anything so as to do anything other than what knowledge bids him to do, but rather prudence is competent to come to the person's aid?"

"It is," he said, "just as you say, Socrates, in my opinion. And at the
352d   same time, it's shameful for me of all people to deny that wisdom and knowledge are most excellent[169] of all human things."

"What you say is noble, at any rate," I said, "and true.

"You know, then, that the many among human beings aren't persuaded by me and you but contend that, though many know what the best things are, they are unwilling to do them—despite their being able to do them—but do other things instead. And indeed all those I've asked what in the world the cause of this is contend that

168. *Eidos*: see n. 107.
169. Or, "superior," "strongest" (*kratiston*).

those who do these things are overcome by pleasure or pain, or are
352e overpowered by one of those things I was just now speaking of."

"For I think, Socrates," he said, "that people[170] say many other
things that aren't correct either."

"Come, then, attempt with me to persuade people and to teach
them what this experience of theirs is, which they say is being over-
353a come by pleasures and, on account of them, not doing the best things,
though they know what they are. For perhaps when we say, 'What
you say isn't correct, you people, but you are mistaken,'[171] they
might ask us, 'Protagoras and Socrates, if this experience isn't one of
being overcome by pleasure, what in the world is it, and what do you
contend that it is? You two tell us.'"

"Why, Socrates, ought we to investigate the opinion of the many
among human beings, who say whatever happens to occur to them?"
353b "I think," I said, "that this has some bearing for us on discovering
something about courage, namely what in the world its relation to
the other parts of virtue is. So if it seems best to you to stick with what
we just now resolved upon, that I take the lead in the way that I, at
least, think will most nobly make it manifest, follow along. But if you
don't want to, and if it's agreeable to you, I'm willing to let it be."

"But what you say is correct," he said. "Complete it as you began it."
353c "Well, then," I said, "if they should ask us once again, 'So what do
you[172] assert this is, which we used to say is being overcome by pleasures?' For my part I'd say to them the following: 'Listen; we'll try to
tell you, Protagoras and I. Do you assert, you people, that anything
else happens to you in these circumstances—when often, for example, you are overpowered by food and drink and sex, which are pleasures—than that you know they are base[173] and yet you partake of
them nonetheless?'"

"They would say that that's so."

"So then, we would ask them again, you and I: 'In what respect do
you assert that they are base? Is it because they supply this immedi-
353d ate pleasure and because each of them is pleasant? Or because they

---

170. Literally, "the human beings," here and throughout this section. The phrase in this context is equivalent to "the many" (*hoi polloi*) and shares its negative connotation.
171. Or, perhaps, "are lying."
172. The plural "you," here and throughout this section.
173. The word (*ponēros*) can mean bad or useless but also worthless (in a moral sense) or
evil.

subsequently cause illnesses and poverty and supply many other such things? Or even if they supply none of these things later on but just cause delight, would they nonetheless be bad, simply because they cause this delight in one way or another?' Do we suppose, Protagoras, that they would give any other answer than that they are bad, not as regards the production of the immediate pleasure itself,

353e   but on account of what subsequently arises, illnesses and the rest?"

"I think," Protagoras said, "that the many would say this in response."

"'So by creating illnesses, they cause distress, and by creating poverty, they cause distress?' They would agree, as I think." Protagoras agreed.

"'Then does it appear to you, you people, as both Protagoras and I contend, that these are bad on account of nothing other than that they ultimately issue in distress and deprive one of other pleasures?'

354a   Would they agree?" That was the opinion of us both. "If then we should further ask them the contrary point: 'You people who say that goods, in turn, are distressing, don't you mean the following sorts of things: physical exercises, for example, and military campaigns, and treatments administered by physicians that involve burning and cutting and drugs and restricted diets—these are on the one hand good, but on the other distressing?' Would they say that that is so?" That was his opinion too.

354b   "'Do you call them good, then, in respect to this, because they cause extreme discomfort and pain immediately, or because subsequently health arises from them and the good condition of bodies, the preservation of cities, empire over others, and wealth?' They would say that that is so, as I think." That was his opinion too.

"'Are these things good on account of anything other than that they ultimately issue in pleasures and the release from and averting of pains? Or can you state any other end with a view to which you

354c   call them good, other than pleasures and pains?' They would say no, as I think."

"That's my opinion too," Protagoras said.

"'Then do you pursue pleasure on the grounds that it is good and flee pain on the grounds that it is bad?'" That was his opinion.

"'So you believe this to be bad—pain—and pleasure good, since you say that feeling delight itself is bad whenever it deprives one of greater pleasures than the ones it itself provides, or whenever it sup-

354d   plies greater pains than the pleasures inherent in it. For if you call feeling delight itself bad in some other respect and with a view to some other end, you could tell us as well. But you won't be able to.' "

"Nor could they, in my opinion," Protagoras said.

" 'Then this holds in the same way again in regard to the feeling of pain itself, doesn't it? Do you call feeling pain itself good when it either delivers one from greater pains than those inherent in it or supplies greater pleasures than pains? For if when you call feeling pain 354e itself good, you look to some end other than the one I speak of, you can tell us. But you won't be able to.' "

"What you say is true," Protagoras said.

" 'Well, then,' " I said, " 'if you should ask me again, you people, "For the sake of what in the world are you speaking about this at such length and in so many ways?" for my part I would say: Please excuse me. For, to begin with, it isn't easy to demonstrate what in the world that which you call "being overcome by pleasures" is. In addition, all the demonstrations are bound up with this. But it is still possible, even now, to retract a step,[174] if in some way you can state that the 355a good is something other than the pleasant, or that the bad is something other than the distressing. Or is it enough for you to live out your life pleasantly, in the absence of pains? If it is enough, and you can't state that the good or the bad is anything other than that which does not issue in these, then listen to what comes next.

" 'For I assert that, this being the case, your argument becomes laughable when you say that although a human being often knows that the bad things are bad, he does them nonetheless, it being possible for him not to, because he is led by pleasures and is dumbstruck 355b by them. And again, in turn, you say that a human being, though he knows the good things, is unwilling to do them on account of his being overcome by immediate pleasures.

" 'And that these things are laughable will be quite clear if we don't make use of many names at once—"pleasant" and "distressing," "good" and "bad." Rather, since these two things have come to sight, let's address them by these two names, first "good" and "bad," then 355c in turn "pleasant" and "distressing." Given this, let's say that although a human being knows that the bad things are bad, he does them nonetheless. If then someone asks us, "On account of what?" we will say, "Because he's overcome." "By what?" he will ask us. And it's no longer possible for us to say, "By pleasure," for it has taken on

---

174. The verb Socrates here uses (*anathesthai*) suggests taking back a move in a board game.

another name—"the good" instead of "the pleasant." So let's answer
him by saying, "Overcome." "By what?" he will say. "By the good,
by Zeus!" we will say. Now if our questioner happens to be inso-
355d lent,[175] he'll laugh and say: "You speak of a laughable thing, if someone does bad things, though he knows them to be bad and doesn't
have to do them, because he's overcome by the good things.

"'"Do the good things," he will say, "not deserve to win within us
over the bad things, or do they deserve to?" It's clear that we will say
in response, "They don't deserve to. Otherwise, the one who we assert is overcome by pleasures would not have erred." "And in what
respect," he will perhaps say, "are the good things undeserving vis-
à-vis the bad, or the bad vis-à-vis the good? Is it in any other respect
than when some are larger, others smaller? Or more numerous, on
355e the one hand, and fewer, on the other?" We won't be able to say anything other than this. "So it's clear," he will say, "that by this 'being
overcome' is meant[176] taking greater bad things in place of fewer
goods." So much, then, for that.'

"'Let's apply the names "pleasant" and "distressing" again to
these same things, and let's say that a human being does what we
were calling "the bad things"—but now let's call them "the distressing things"—although he knows that they do produce distress, be-
356a cause he's overcome by pleasures; it's clear that they don't deserve to
win. And what other lack of desert[177] is there for pleasure in regard
to pain, except excess and deficiency in one or the other? And these
occur when [the pleasures and pains] are greater and smaller than
one another, more numerous and fewer, more and less. For if someone should say, "But, Socrates, immediate pleasure differs a great
deal from subsequent pleasure as well as pain," I for my part would
say, "Surely not in any way other than in pleasure and pain?" For no
356b other way is possible. But like a human being good at weighing,
adding up the pleasures and adding up the pains, putting the near-
ness and farness in the balance as well, say which of the two is greater.
For if you weigh pleasures against pleasures, you must always
choose those that are greater and more numerous; if pains against

175. Or, "arrogant," "hubristic."
176. Reading *legetai* with the mss. The emendation adopted by Burnet and Croiset (*legete*)
would read in translation: "you [plural] mean by this 'being overcome.'"
177. The reading of the mss., defended by Adam and Adam. Croiset, following Schleiermacher, reads, "And what other desert [deserving] is there."

pains, the fewer and smaller; and if you weigh pleasures against pains and the distressing things are outstripped by pleasures, whether those near are less than those at a distance or those at a distance are less than those near, you must carry out that action in which these [greater pleasures] are found. But if the pleasures are out-

356c   stripped by the distressing things, you mustn't carry out that action. Are these things not so,' I would say, 'you people?' I know that they couldn't say otherwise." He too was of this opinion.

" 'Since this is so, answer me the following,' I will say. 'Do the same magnitudes appear to you by sight to be bigger when nearby but smaller from far away, or not?' "

"They will say that they do."

" 'And similarly with thicknesses and numbers? And equal sounds too are greater when nearby but weaker from far away?' "

"They would say that that's so."

356d   " 'If then our acting well[178] were to consist in this, in our grasping and acting in accord with the great distances and avoiding the small distances and not acting in accord with them, what means of saving[179] our life would have come to sight? The art of measuring or the power of appearances?[180] Or wouldn't this latter cause us, as we saw, to wander about and change our minds back and forth many times about the same things and go back on our decision when it comes to both our actions and our choosing things that are great and small? Wouldn't the art of measuring, on the other hand, have rendered this apparition powerless and, by having made clear the truth, would it

356e   not have set our soul at peace, fixed before the truth, and have saved our life?' Would the people agree, in light of these things, that it is the measuring art that saves us, or another one?"

"The measuring art," he agreed.

" 'And what if the saving of our life depended on our choosing odd and even, when we had to choose correctly the greater and the lesser, taking either each in relation to itself or the one in relation to the other, whether up close or at a distance? What would save our life? Would

357a   it not be knowledge? And would this not be a certain art of measuring, since in fact the art pertains to excess and deficiency? And since

178. Or, "faring well."
179. Or, "preserving," here and throughout.
180. Literally, "of the appearance" or "of that which appears."

this concerns odd and even, what else would this be other than arithmetic?' Would the people agree with us or not?" It was Protagoras' opinion too that they would agree.

" 'Well, then, you people, since the saving of our life manifestly depends on the correct choice of pleasure and pain—of more and less, 357b greater and smaller, more distant and nearer—doesn't it appear, to begin with, that it is an art of measuring, it being an inquiry into excess and deficiency and equality regarding the two?'"

"Necessarily."

" 'And since it is a measuring art, then doubtless it is necessarily an art and knowledge.'"

"They too will say that that's so."

" 'Well, whatever this art and knowledge is, we'll investigate later. But that it is knowledge—this much is enough for the demonstration that Protagoras and I must give concerning the things you asked us 357c about. And you put your question to us, if you remember, when we were agreeing with one another that there is nothing superior[181] to knowledge but that wherever this is present it always overpowers both pleasure and all other things. But you asserted that pleasure often overpowers even a human being possessed of knowledge, and when we didn't agree with you, you then asked us, "Protagoras and Socrates, if this experience is not one of being overcome by pleasure, what in the world is it and what do you assert it to be? Tell us." If we 357d had then said straight off that it is ignorance, you would have ridiculed us. But now, if you ridicule us, you'll be ridiculing yourselves as well. For you too have agreed that those who err in choosing pleasures and pains—and these are what are good and bad—do so through a lack of knowledge; and not only of knowledge but of that knowledge which you've further agreed to previously is the art of measuring.[182] And you yourselves know, surely, that an erring ac- 357e tion without knowledge is done through ignorance, with the result that this is what being overcome by pleasure is: the greatest ignorance, for which Protagoras here claims he is a physician, as do Prodicus and Hippias. But on account of supposing that it is something

---

181. Or, "stronger" (*kreittōn*).
182. The reading of Burnet, following two principal mss., defended by Adam and Adam and Manuwald; Croiset reads, with slight ms. authority: "and not only through a lack of knowledge but of what you further agreed to previously is the art of measuring."

other than ignorance, neither you yourselves [go][183] to these sophists here as the teachers of these things, nor do you send your sons to them, on the grounds that it isn't something teachable. Instead, because you're concerned about your money and so don't give it to them, you act badly both privately and publicly.'

358a   "These are the answers we would have given to the many. But together with Protagoras I ask you, Hippias and Prodicus—for you[184] may share in the argument—is what I'm saying true or false in your opinion?" It was the opinion of all that what had been said was true to an extraordinary degree. "You agree, then," I said, "that the pleasant is good, the distressing bad. And I beg forgiveness from Prodicus here concerning the distinction between the names. For whether you say 'pleasant' or 'pleasing' or 'delightful,' or on whatever basis and

358b   however you delight in naming things of this sort, best Prodicus, answer me with a view to what I mean." Prodicus then laughed and agreed, as did the others.

"What then, men," I said, "about the following sort of thing: are all the actions that lead to this, to living free of pain and pleasantly, aren't they noble?[185] And is a noble deed both good and advantageous?" That was the opinion. "If then," I said, "the pleasant is good, no one who either knows or supposes that other things are better than those that he is doing, things that are also possible, then does these [infe-

358c   rior] things, when it is possible to do the better. And this 'being overcome by oneself' is nothing other than ignorance, and overpowering oneself is nothing other than wisdom." This was the opinion of all. "So what then? Do you mean by ignorance the following sort of thing: having a false opinion and stating falsehoods[186] concerning matters of great importance?" This too was the opinion of all.

"Is anything else the case," I said, "than that nobody willingly advances toward the bad things or toward things he supposes to be bad,

358d   nor is this, as seems likely, a part of human nature, namely to be willing to go toward things one supposes to be bad instead of the good things? And whenever one is compelled to choose one of two bad

---

183. The text would appear to be corrupt, for no verb is present; I supply what I take to be missing.
184. The plural "you."
185. The mss. add at this point the words "and advantageous," but the modern editors, following Schleiermacher, delete the phrase.
186. Or, "lying."

things, no one will choose the greater one when it's possible to choose the lesser?" All these things were so in the opinion of us all.

"What then?" I said. "Do you call something 'dread' and 'fear,' and—I say this to you, Prodicus—is it what in fact I mean by it? I say that this is a certain expectation of something bad, whether you call it 'fear' or 'dread.'" In the opinion of Protagoras and Hippias, this was what "dread" and "fear" are; but in Prodicus' opinion, it was

358e "dread" but not "fear." "But, Prodicus," I said, "it doesn't matter. This, however, does: if what came before is true, will any human being be willing to advance toward things he is afraid of, when it is possible for him to advance toward things he is not afraid of? Or is that impossible on the basis of what's been agreed to? For it was agreed that that which he is afraid of he believes to be bad, and that which he believes to be bad, no one advances toward or accepts willingly."

359a This too was the opinion of all.

"Given these things, then, Prodicus and Hippias," I said, "let Protagoras here defend for us the correctness of the answers he gave at first—though not his very first ones. For he said then that none of the five parts of virtue is such as any other, each having its own particular power. So I don't mean this, but rather what he said later on. For later on he said that four of them are reasonably comparable to one another but that one differs very much from the others, namely

359b courage, and he said that I would know this from the following piece of evidence: 'You will discover, Socrates, human beings who are very impious and very unjust and very licentious and very unlearned, but very courageous. By this you will know that courage differs very much from the other parts of virtue.' And at the time I was immediately filled with a great deal of wonder at the answer, and still more so when I went through these things together with you.[187] And so I asked him if he says the courageous are bold, and he said, 'They're

359c even eager.' Do you recall giving these answers, Protagoras?" I said. He agreed that he did.

"Come, then," I said, "tell us, for what do you say the courageous are eager? What the cowards are in fact eager for?" He said no. "Then for other things."

"Yes," he said.

187. The plural "you."

"Do the cowards advance toward things they feel bold about, the courageous toward terrible things?"

"So it is said, Socrates, by people."[188]

"What you say is true," I said. "But that's not what I'm asking. Instead, what do *you* assert the courageous are eager for? For terrible things, believing them to be terrible, or for things that are not terrible?"

"But that, at least," he said, "was just now demonstrated to be impossible in the arguments you were making."

"This too that you say," I said, "is true. As a result, if this was correctly demonstrated, no one advances toward things he believes to be terrible, since being overcome by oneself was discovered to be ignorance." He agreed.

"But then all in turn advance toward things they feel bold about, both cowards and the courageous, and in this respect, at least, the cowards and the courageous advance toward the same things."

"And yet, Socrates," he said, "the cowards and the courageous advance toward entirely contrary things: for example, the latter are willing to go to war; the former are not willing."

"Is it noble to go, or shameful?" I said.

"Noble," he said.

"Then if in fact it is noble, we agreed in what came before that it is also good, for all noble actions, we agreed, were good."

"What you say is true; and I, at least, am always of that opinion."

"Correctly so," I said. "But which of the two do you assert is unwilling to go to war, it being noble and good to do so?"

"The cowards," he said.

"Then if in fact it is noble and good, is it also pleasant?" I said.

"That was agreed to, at any rate," he said.

"Although they know this, then, the cowards are unwilling to advance toward that which is nobler[189] and better and more pleasant?"

"But if we agree to this too," he said, "we'll destroy the previous agreements."

"And what about the courageous man? Doesn't he advance toward that which is nobler and better and more pleasant?"

"It's necessary," he said, "to agree."

---

188. Literally, "by the human beings" (see nn. 26 and 170).
189. Reading, with the modern editors, Stephanus' emendation; the mss. read: "that which is noble and better and more pleasant?"

360b   "In general, then, the courageous don't have shameful fears, whenever they are afraid, nor do they have shameful boldness?"

"True," he said.

"And if they aren't shameful, aren't they noble?" He agreed. "And if noble, also good?"

"Yes."

"So then the cowards and the rash and the madmen, by contrast, have both shameful fears and shameful boldness?" He agreed. "And do they feel boldness when it comes to shameful and bad things on account of anything other than lack of knowledge and ignorance?"

"That's so," he said.

360c   "What, then? Do you call that on account of which the cowards are cowards 'cowardice' or 'courage'?"

"For my part, 'cowardice,'" he said.

"And weren't the cowards manifestly such on account of the ignorance of what's terrible?"

"Certainly," he said.

"So they are cowards on account of this ignorance?" He agreed. "And that on account of which they are cowards is agreed by you to be cowardice?" He said that that was so. "So then the ignorance of what's terrible and what isn't terrible would be cowardice?" He nodded.

"But surely courage is the contrary of cowardice," I said. He said that that was so.

"So the wisdom pertaining to what's terrible and what isn't terrible is the contrary of the ignorance of these things?" Here he nodded again.

"And the ignorance of these things, cowardice?" At this he nodded, but with great reluctance.

"So the wisdom pertaining to what's frightening and what isn't is courage, it being the contrary of ignorance of these things?" Here he was no longer willing even to nod and was silent. And I said, "What's this, Protagoras? You neither affirm nor deny what I'm asking?"

"Finish it off yourself," he said.

360e   "I'll ask you just one more thing," I said, "whether it is still your opinion, as it was at first, that there are some human beings who are very unlearned,[190] on the one hand, and very courageous, on the other."

190. Or, "ignorant": it is related to the word translated at 360d as "ignorance."

"In my opinion, Socrates," he said, "my being the one to answer just serves your love of victory. So I'll gratify you and say that in my opinion it's impossible on the basis of what's been agreed to."

"But I'm not asking all these things," I said, "for the sake of anything other than my wish to investigate how in the world things stand in regard to virtue and what in the world virtue itself is. For I

361a know that, once this becomes manifest, that about which each of us, you and I, has drawn out a long speech would become especially clear—I saying that virtue isn't something teachable, you that it is something teachable. And in my opinion the recent outcome of our speeches is, like a human being, accusing and ridiculing us; and should it attain a voice, it would say: 'You two are strange, Socrates and Protagoras. For you, on the one hand, were saying in what came before that virtue isn't something teachable, but now you are urging

361b things that contradict yourself by attempting to demonstrate that all things are knowledge—justice and moderation and courage—in which manner virtue would most of all appear to be something teachable. For if virtue were something other than knowledge, as Protagoras was attempting to say, it clearly wouldn't be something teachable. But now, if it will appear to be entirely knowledge, as you are urging, Socrates, it'll be a wonder if it isn't teachable. But Protagoras, on the other hand, set it down previously as something teachable, but now by contrast he resembles someone urging that it

361c appear to be almost anything other than knowledge. And in this way it would least of all be something teachable.'

"So I, Protagoras, seeing all these things in such terrible confusion, I'm altogether eager that they become clear, and I'd like, once we've thoroughly gone through these things, to go through also the matter of what virtue is and investigate once again whether it is something teachable or isn't something teachable. Otherwise, perhaps that fa-

361d mous Epimetheus may deceive and baffle us in our investigation, just as he neglected us in his distribution, as you assert. Prometheus was more pleasing to me in the myth than was Epimetheus; and, making use of him and exercising forethought[191] for the sake of my own life as a whole, I am concerned with all these things. And should you be willing, then, as I was saying at the beginning as well, I would very gladly make a thorough investigation of these things together with you."

---

191. The word (*promēthoumenos*) recalls the name of Prometheus (see n. 56).

And Protagoras said, "I praise your eagerness, Socrates, and the course of the arguments. And I think that in other respects too I'm not 361e a bad human being, but least of all human beings am I envious. For indeed I've said of you to many that I admire you by far the most of those I've happened across, especially those of your age. I say too that I wouldn't wonder if you should take your place among the men held in high regard for wisdom. And we'll go through these things later, whenever you want. But now it's already time to turn to something else."

362a   "But this is what must be done," I said, "if it seems best to you. For it's long been time for me to go where I said, but I stayed to gratify the noble Callias."[192]

Having said and heard these things, we departed.

192. The phrase "noble Callias" contains an alliterative jingle: *Kallia tō kalō*.

On the *Protagoras*

THE OPENING SCENES AND THE PURPOSE OF THE DIALOGUE

The bulk of the *Protagoras* consists of Socrates' report to an unnamed comrade of a conversation he has just had with the famous sophist at the behest of the young and impetuous Hippocrates. Hippocrates has heard (because "all" say it: 310e6) that Protagoras is "wisest at speaking"; and he wishes to become a student of Protagoras, evidently because he believes that acquiring such wisdom or skill himself is essential to fulfilling his political ambition—to his becoming "held in high regard in the city" (310e6–7; 316b10–c1). For his part, Socrates warns Hippocrates that he is about to entrust the education of his soul to a sophist even though he is ignorant of what wise matter the sophist teaches and hence of its worth. And despite his eagerness to study with Protagoras, Hippocrates blushes at the suggestion that he wishes to do so in order to become a sophist himself (312a2; compare 315a4–5); even Hippocrates doubts the respectability of sophistry, however useful it may be.

In these ways the argument and the action of the dialogue indicate its most obvious task: Socrates attempts to uncover, for the sake of Hippocrates, the character and worth of Protagoras' instruction—and indeed to warn him away from it. But as Socrates himself insists, to evaluate the worth of the education Protagoras offers, one must be a knower of the things that benefit and harm the soul or a "physician expert in what pertains to the soul" (313e1–5). If Socrates' critique of Protagoras is to be convincing, then, it must not merely stymie or embarrass the sophist but also

67

demonstrate to us its audience the soundness of the standard or goal to which it looks in doing so. Does the education Protagoras offers meet the Socratic requirements of a good education—whatever these may be? The sophist as educator, especially in his difference from the philosopher, is the theme of the *Protagoras*.

We must wonder, however, whether Socrates' concern for Hippocrates fully explains the conversation before us. After all, it is Socrates who suggests that he and Hippocrates make their way to Protagoras and the other sophists (314b6–c2), just after he has issued a stinging rebuke to Hippocrates for his uninformed desire to do so, and at an important juncture in the dialogue Socrates assures Protagoras that his cross-examinations have as their goal the discovery of the truth about virtue, about a question that perplexes Socrates himself. His conversation with Protagoras is intended to make certain one or more of Socrates' own thoughts, as only conversation with or "testing" of another can do (347c5–349a6; consider also, e.g., 328d8–e1, as well as 357e2–8: Socrates is not consistently concerned with harming the business prospects of the sophists, Protagoras included).

The first impression we receive from the dialogue of Socrates' concern for the moral education of Hippocrates, a concern remarkable not least for its patient forbearance, is due in part to the fact that Socrates is addressing or adapting himself throughout to his unnamed comrade (together with certain anonymous others: 310a2, 5–7)—to a man who, however well-disposed to Socrates he may be, is more interested in gossip than philosophy (309b2–3, c1–3), is thoroughly conventional in his deference to Homer and his preference for the homegrown over the foreign (309a1–b2, c9–10), and is even less privy to the intellectual happenings in Athens than is Hippocrates: if Hippocrates knew of the arrival of Protagoras a day later than did Socrates, the comrade remains unaware of it on the third day after the fact (compare 310b7–8 with 309d3–4). The comrade assumes the relationship between Socrates and Alcibiades, of which he playfully disapproves, to be a sexual one (309a1–5), and Socrates does not stoop to correct this assumption (consider *Symposium* 219c6–d2 and context). But the account he gives of his attempt to shield Hippocrates from an education at the hands of a sophist would go some way toward protecting him from suspicion that he in any way corrupts the young: he prevents their corruption.

It is true that, after Socrates has succeeded in embarrassing Protagoras by pursuing questions that Protagoras finds annoying—that is, after he has dulled the luster of Protagoras' reputation in the eyes of his potential students—Socrates indicates his intention to leave the get-together (335c3–7).

Yet Socrates stays in fact, and he must have suspected that the mere statement of his intention to leave would elicit the pleas and negotiations it did
elicit and so permit the conversation to continue on terms more agreeable
to him. It is certain that Socrates did not have any pressing matter to attend
to elsewhere, as he claims to have, for upon finally leaving Callias' home
he happens upon his unnamed comrade and repeats the just-completed
conversation in all but its entirety (compare 335c5–6 and 362a2–4 with
310a2–5; for the omissions, see 314c3–7, 316a6–7, and 348b1). And Socrates
never indicates what effect any of this had on Hippocrates (or for that
matter on his comrade). Could it be that Socrates' deepest concerns, the
question or questions he wishes to examine together with Protagoras, are
presented in the guise of his concern for the moral education of Hippocrates, or at any rate that the latter is strictly subordinate to the former?
If this is so, then Socrates demonstrates before our eyes his "good counsel
concerning his own affairs," which issues in a manifest or ostentatious concern for the affairs of others.

As Socrates and Hippocrates arrive outside the home of Callias, the two
complete a conversation, the substance of which Socrates refrains from reporting to the comrade but which leads the feisty eunuch who does hear it
to conclude that they too are sophists: to the mostly (but not entirely) uninformed, Socrates and the sophists are as one. With the begrudging com-
pliance of the eunuch, Socrates gains entry and immediately surveys the
scene inside: he first sees Protagoras, who enjoys the greatest number of
followers, including very prominent Athenians (Callias, the two sons of
Pericles, Charmides) as well as a good many foreigners; then Hippias with
a smaller retinue that includes two sometime members of the Socratic circle (Eryximachus and Phaedrus); and finally Prodicus, who is also with a
mix of Athenians (including the young Agathon) and foreigners.

Quoting from Odysseus' remarks in the course of his famous passage
through the House of Hades, the Greek underworld, Socrates implies that
Hippias is akin to Heracles, Prodicus to Tantalus, and, more generally, the
House of Callias to the House of Hades—and not without reason, for Callias and Hades enjoy the dubious distinction of having kept company with
their respective wives and the mothers of their wives.[1] Perhaps because he
is distracted by Protagoras' delightfully comic chorus, Socrates neither describes Protagoras himself (beyond his capacity to bewitch people with his

---

1. See Andocides, *On the Mysteries* 124–27, and Leo Strauss, *Xenophon's Socratic Discourse*
(Ithaca: Cornell University Press, 1970), 157–58.

voice) nor indicates the subject matter of his discourse to which all are so attentive; Protagoras' voice surely fails to bewitch Socrates. Only in the case of Prodicus—a man "altogether wise and divine"—does Socrates make known his (unfulfilled) desire to hear what is being said (consider also 340e8–341a4), and only in the second and central case does Socrates state the subject matter of the discussions: Hippias is giving detailed responses to certain astronomical questions pertaining to "nature and the things aloft" (315c5–6; note also the mention of astronomy at 318d9–e4). Coming in just behind Socrates are Critias and Alcibiades, the latter being the supposed object of Socrates' affection (316a6–b2; 390a5). In this closely guarded and rather exotic underworld, filled to capacity with sophists and their devotees, foreigners with their foreign ways mix easily with the best of Athenian society or its youth—including a budding poet (Agathon), two future tyrants (Critias, Charmides), and a philosopher. In the unconventional and even decadent atmosphere created by the profligacy of Callias (*Apology of Socrates* 20a4–6 and Xenophon, *Symposium* 1.5), it would seem that the hold of the merely homegrown ways or customs (*nomoi*) is loosened considerably (consider 309c9–10). Here apparently one can enjoy the freedom necessary to discuss openly the gravest matters, including "the things aloft" and their fixed "nature": here the things aloft are assumed to be not divine but natural—perhaps stones and earth, for example (*Apology of Socrates* 26d1–5 and context). And here one can venture the view, as Hippias does later on, that those present are governed and united by nature and not at all by the "tyrant" *nomos* (337c6–e2).

PROTAGORAS' TEACHING

The "sophisticated" atmosphere we are thus introduced to makes all the more striking both the extreme caution with which Protagoras speaks throughout and the delicacy, marked by forethought, with which Socrates first approaches him (316c5; 318d5–7). Even here, in what is at most a semipublic gathering, Protagoras' first concern is with the nature of the audience he is to address (316b3–4; compare 317c6–d1), and he is prompted by that concern to offer to the restricted audience of Socrates and Hippocrates some important reflections on the great danger to which his practice of sophistry subjects him and, in particular, on the difference between him and his predecessors in grappling with that danger. For whereas all previous sophists endeavored to conceal, by means of one sort of "cloak" or another, the very fact that they were sophists, the aptly named Protagoras ("first to speak out") is perfectly open about his being a sophist.

But for all his distance from the earlier sophists with their apparently clumsy and even counterproductive efforts at concealment—effective only with the many, who "perceive as it were nothing" (317a4–5), as distinguished from the powerful few—Protagoras nowhere claims to have removed the necessity dictating the use of such concealment. On the contrary, Protagoras' openness is itself a precaution (317b5) meant to protect him, and he mentions but fails to specify certain other means of concealment that keep him from suffering harm as a result of agreeing that he is a sophist (317b6). Put another way, Protagoras' openness is only a partial openness and it too is motivated by the need for self-protection. As the results of Socrates' cross-examination of Hippocrates already suggest, Protagoras is frank about the fact *that* he teaches but not about *what* he teaches (consider also 352a8–b1).

Only under pressure from Socrates does Protagoras state more or less candidly the nature of his instruction: "The subject in question is good counsel concerning one's own affairs—how he might best manage his own household—and, concerning the affairs of the city, how he might be the most powerful in carrying out and speaking about the city's affairs" (318e5–319a2). The successful student of Protagoras, then, will of course benefit himself by managing his private affairs well, but Protagoras leaves unclear the end with a view to which his student will exercise preeminent power in the city: will he be guided by the desire to benefit the city or himself? It is certainly true that Socrates immediately imposes on Protagoras the most respectable interpretation of his remarks possible—to the effect that Protagoras teaches the political art and good citizenship, words that had never passed Protagoras' lips—just as it is true that Protagoras happily concedes this to be what he publicly pronounces or "professes" (319a6–7). But since we have just been alerted to the dangerous character of Protagoras' activity, to the "ill will and hostile plots" to which it can give rise (316d3), as well as to his necessary recourse to arts of concealment, we must be especially wary of becoming, like "the many," his dupes. Could it be that Protagoras promises to teach his students how to benefit themselves in matters public as well as private, or that he teaches them how to gain preeminent power in order to use the common good for the sake of their own good? Is not Protagoras' claim to bestow the greatest political power on his students—that is, on anyone who can pay the tuition (consider 316b8–9), however unpromising his nature[2]—at least a little troubling? All this suggests that when Socrates turns to raise the question of whether such good citizenship is in fact teachable, we must keep on the table the prior and more fundamental question of precisely *what* Protagoras teaches.

To support his view that the political art or good citizenship (319a4–5, 8–9) cannot be taught, Socrates offers two pieces of evidence. First, when some technical matter requiring expert advice arises, the democratic assembly of Athens refuses to hear from any but the acknowledged experts. Whenever deliberation is required concerning the city's management more generally, however, any and every citizen is permitted to speak because—according to Socrates—all believe such political expertise to be unteachable and thus all citizens to be equally capable (or incapable?) of offering it; no special expertise in politics is attainable through instruction and hence it cannot be demanded. If the evidence Socrates offers is uncontroversial, his interpretation of it surely is. For would not the Athenians claim rather that all citizens are equally capable of giving political advice because all—all gentlemen, at least—not only possess the relevant expertise but also can and do teach it to their fellow citizens (see, e.g., *Meno* 92e3–6 and context)?

Socrates would appear to be on more solid ground when he notes, in the second place, that even "our wisest and best citizens" cannot bestow on their own kin the expertise they possess, an expertise he now, and for the first time, calls "virtue" (319e2; also 320a3, b5). Pericles, for example, has as yet been unable to educate his young ward Cleinias, let alone turn him into another Pericles. It is clear on reflection that Socrates has in mind two quite different conceptions of political excellence, the one characteristic of the good or dutiful citizen, the other of the greatest statesmen: "good citizenship" differs from "the political art" at its peak, and if the latter cannot be taught, does not every city claim, at least, to teach the former? Or—since the teachability of virtue proves to rest on its being knowledge in the strict sense (*epistēmē*: 361a6–c2; *Meno* 87b1–c7)—does Socrates here mean to cast doubt on the rationality of what is conveyed in and through the "educa-

---

2. Compare 316b9–10 with 10–11: Socrates vouches only for Hippocrates' wealth and his political ambition, not for the opinion pertaining to the boy's nature. And Protagoras shows no interest in discerning the suitability of that nature for instruction (consider 327b7–c1 as well as 351a3 and b2: Protagoras is of course aware of the importance of one's nature in making true progress).

tion" to citizenship? Socrates' challenge to Protagoras concerning the teachability of virtue certainly undermines the sophist's business prospects, but it also introduces the question of what properly constitutes virtue and whether in all its various forms or guises it is rational and hence teachable.

Protagoras' lengthy response to Socrates includes the complex myth of Prometheus and Epimetheus for which the dialogue is probably best known. We limit ourselves to some preliminary observations. To begin with, the myth indicated is but one part of a long speech that also contains an argument, a *logos,* properly speaking (320c6–7; 324d6–7; 328c3), and the ostensible purpose of the long speech as a whole is of course to prove that virtue is teachable and that Protagoras himself can teach it. But Protagoras also achieves two different (if related) ends by means of it: he intimates to his potential students in the room, Alcibiades, Critias, and Charmides among them, the truth of what he (truly) teaches, even as he shores up the conventional opinions he and his successful students will exploit in their quest to become "most powerful." For it seems that Protagoras believes of Zeus not only that he exists but also that he is a divinely beneficent lawgiver—a Zeus who cares for the whole human race, who in his care for us gave justice and shame to all, and who made political life possible by setting it down as a law that anyone who does not share in these will be killed on the grounds that he is an illness in the city (322d1–5). But in truth—even if one ignores the fact that all this is conveyed in what is explicitly a *myth* largely of Protagoras' creation—the details of it suggest a rather dark picture of the human condition. Zeus cares for the human race; i.e., he is indifferent to the fate of individuals. His concern for the race extends only so far that it not perish *entirely* (321a2, b6 and especially 322c1); and such care as he exercises takes the form of entrusting our well-being to two bunglers, for even the prudence of Prometheus ("Forethought") does not prevent him from allowing the erring Epimetheus ("Afterthought") to distribute the various capacities or powers to all creatures (320d4–8). The world is fundamentally "Epimethean": thought follows rather than precedes creation. The only comforts we have were invented by us through arts of our own devising; and we attained fire, the prerequisite of their development, only through an act of rebellion against the gods for which, "it is said," Prometheus was later made to pay (322a1–2). Our true condition is one of utter abandonment. There is only the natural order that (at most) favors the continuation of the human species. Even the brute animals are better off by nature than we are, for in addition to possessing natural defenses, they easily come together to form communities of a kind, whereas we fell to slaughtering one another almost as soon as we drew together. And to restrain ourselves, to make political life possible, it was necessary not that Zeus actually become a lawgiver but that "all" believe him to have done so.

Protagoras' myth thus puts before our eyes the kind of conviction that human beings must have if they will restrain themselves sufficiently to form lasting political communities. But this is not quite correct: Protagoras notes as if in passing that not all are just in fact and that it would be madness *to admit to* one's injustice or to fail *to pretend* to possess justice (323a5–c2). He does not say that it would be madness *to be* unjust, and he omits mention of the fatal wrath of Zeus extending to such unjust dissemblers. Political societies require not the universal agreement as to the goodness of justice and the divine sanctions attending its violation but the near-universal agreement; political society will endure perfectly well, in other words, if only a few understand the truth about justice and especially if these few also happen to be clever enough to conceal their true thoughts (consider 310e5–7; 317b5–c1) by "speaking with god" (compare 317b7), for example, or by using such devices as myth and poetry (339a3–6).

The subsequent exchanges between Socrates and Protagoras confirm the suspicion that Protagoras is a teacher of injustice. He teaches, that is, that the unjust way of life is superior to the just life, that the happy few exploit the ignorant many, and that the only true virtues are wisdom and courage.[3] According to Protagoras' account of it, "political virtue" (323a6–7, b2, 324a1) is limited to moderation, justice, and piety, or to what might be called ordinary decency, and the so-called education necessary to instill it consists of exhortations, forced memorization, threats, and even beatings: " 'Do these things!' 'Don't do those!' " (325d5 and context; the *beliefs* of the Athenians and indeed of all human beings pertaining to virtue properly belong to Protagoras' myth rather than to his *logos*: see 322d5–324d1 and the transition at 324d6–7). This is not the education Protagoras offers, of course, but is rather what everyone receives initially at the hands of the law, of *nomos* broadly understood (consider 326c7–d8, which is the climax of this section); by thus instilling justice, the altogether human law accom-

---

3. Note the transition at 329e5–330a2 and the absence to that point of wisdom and courage from Protagoras' account of "political virtue." (The references to "technical wisdom," "the wisdom pertaining to one's livelihood [*bios*]," and "political wisdom" in this context [321d1–5] do not constitute exceptions to this; as for the mention of cowardice at 326c1, consider pp. 80–82.)

plishes the task Protagoras had initially assigned to Zeus. Such an "education" never mentions, because it has absolutely nothing to do with, wisdom, "the greatest of the virtues" according to Protagoras (330a2; 352d1–3). In fact it is this mere habituation to unthinking obedience, to preferring the city's good to one's own, that Protagoras' instruction must undo—carefully but surely.

In accord with this, when Socrates asks Protagoras whether the individual virtues are parts of a whole, either as bits of gold are part of gold or as mouth, nose, eyes, and ears are parts of the whole that is the face, Protagoras replies without hesitation that the latter is the case. He does so because "the virtues"—justice, moderation, and piety on the one hand, wisdom and courage on the other—prove to be distinct from one another in a way that the former image does not permit: as Protagoras admits, in an (almost) unguarded moment, "many are courageous but unjust, and there are those who are just, in turn, but not wise" (329e5–6). Courage and injustice can go together—successful bank robbers, for example—and justice can go together with a lack of wisdom or indeed foolishness (consider 332a4–6). The crucial question is thus alluded to: is the combination "wise," "courageous," and "unjust" a possible one? More sharply stated, might the wise *as such* be unjust? Socrates tries, mostly unsuccessfully, to force Protagoras to concede that all the virtues are one inasmuch as justice is or is most akin to piety, wisdom to moderation, and, finally, justice (= piety) to moderation (= wisdom). Such begrudging agreement as Socrates is able to wrest from Protagoras results less from the cogency of his arguments here[4] than from their extremely sensitive subject matter: as Socrates orchestrates things, Protagoras would have to agree that piety is unjust and justice impious (331a6–b1), for example, were he openly to oppose him. Yet Socrates' failure to secure unambiguous agreement to the proposition that all the virtues are one means in the context that indeed the wise may not be just, and Protagoras finally asserts, under heavy pressure from Socrates and not of course in his own name, that it *is* a mark of moderation—hence of thinking well, of deliberating well, of faring well, hence of possessing for oneself the good or advantageous things—to commit in-

---

4. The argument that wisdom and moderation must be the same thing, for example, depends on the unproved assertion that each thing has only one contrary (332c8–9 and context); that Socrates elsewhere holds moderation to have two contraries (foolishness and licentiousness) appears from *Gorgias* 507a5–7; note also the otherwise peculiar plural at *Protagoras* 332d4.

justice. No wonder, then, that this line of argument immediately precedes the first breakdown of the conversation and strikes Protagoras as "annoying" (333d2; compare also 332a2).

Socrates' initial question as to what a student will learn from Protagoras culminates in, because it is most honestly answered by, this exchange. It also prompts Protagoras to make a rather angry outburst concerning his understanding of the good that is preceded by his first oath or curse in the dialogue (333d10–334c7). Protagoras stresses not only that "the good" must be judged in reference to the nature or needs of a given thing, but also, and for that very reason, that what is good or bad, advantageous or harmful, is extraordinarily complex—manure, for example, being highly advantageous to mature plants but harmful to young ones. For his part, Socrates notes only that lengthy speeches make him forget the question at issue (334c8–d1). Shortly thereafter, Socrates stands up as though to leave. The threat of his departure prompts the future tyrant Critias to strike a moderate compromise between Callias' proposal and Alcibiades' counterproposal, although it is Socrates' own amendment—that Protagoras should pose questions to him, who will answer briefly and then pose questions again to Protagoras—that carries the day. For all the applause that Protagoras wins from his audience (334c7–8), Socrates proves to be a master at getting the whole of the crowd on his side (338e2–3): Socrates too is a clever speaker, one not above using such devices as flattery, for example (compare 338b4–c6 with d6–e2).

The Unity of Virtue: Pittacus and Simonides

With considerable reluctance, Protagoras takes up Socrates' invitation or challenge, and he does so by initiating the discussion of poetry that appears to be a rather baffling, and lengthy, digression (338e6–347a5). Yet Protagoras himself indicates what is at stake: "the question will concern the same thing that you and I are now conversing about, namely virtue." The question of the unity of virtue, of virtue in its relation to wisdom, will somehow remain in play.

Protagoras begins by quoting from the poetry of Simonides, whom he had earlier identified as a crypto-sophist (316d7), to the effect that it is difficult to become a good man. But Protagoras' immediate interest in the ode proves to be less with the substance of the line than with the author's blatant self-contradiction: Simonides states in his own name that it is difficult to become good and then promptly criticizes Pittacus, "a wise man" (339c4; also 343a2), for maintaining essentially the same view. Thus, "whenever he criticizes one who says the same things as he himself does, it is clear that he criticizes himself as well" (339d7–8). Protagoras' immediate reason for speaking of poetry, then, is to air the complaint that one very clever man is criticizing another for holding the same view he does. Now, Protagoras has already indicated that poetry is one means of sophistic concealment (316d6 and context), and we must put two and two together: does Protagoras mean to indicate to Socrates that he knows that Socrates too holds the same view about virtue that he himself does, that it is improper of Socrates to criticize him in this way, and that he had better cease his aggressive cross-examination?

Socrates, for his part, lets us know that Protagoras' blow has hit home, for he is "dizzy and woozy" as a result of Protagoras' statement (and the crowd's reaction to it). Socrates lets us know too that in his opinion a poet who contradicts himself might speak correctly, if not nobly (339b7–10, with the reading of mss. T and W): intentional self-contradiction might well be excusable. Accordingly, the first two of his attempts to free Simonides from the charge of self-contradiction are dismal failures. That is, when Socrates notes that Simonides had said it is difficult *to become* good, whereas Pittacus had used the verb *to be,* Protagoras simply dismisses the resulting view (of Hesiod, but apparently compatible with Simonides') that it is easy to possess virtue: it is the opinion of all human beings that virtue is the most difficult thing of all.

Abandoning his first response without even attempting to defend it, Socrates next suggests that what Simonides meant by "difficult" was in fact "bad": "so for these reasons . . . he also criticizes Pittacus for saying that 'it's difficult to be noble,' just as if he heard him say, 'It's bad to be noble' " (341c3–5). But the difficulty remains: if we suppose that Simonides understood "difficult" to mean "bad" in both his own lines and those of Pittacus, the self-contradiction stands! And far from defending this suggestion, Socrates dismisses it, though not before he has made explicit its impious character (341d6–9). It is striking that Socrates does not avail himself of the obvious difference between Simonides' saying and that of Pittacus: whereas Simonides speaks of becoming *good* (*agathos*), Pittacus speaks of being *noble* (*esthlos*). Since Protagoras takes each man to be saying the same thing, does he thus assume that the good and the noble are identical?

Socrates leaves this assumption unchallenged here. The relation of what is noble to what is good proves to be a "touchy" subject, one to which Socrates will force Protagoras to return.

Socrates' third and final response (342a6–347a5) begins lightheartedly, with a portrait of the exceedingly philosophic Spartans. Yet the official view of virtue now on the table, according to which virtue is one because it is knowledge (wisdom), permits or requires Socrates to describe the Spartans as he does: the Spartans are exceedingly virtuous; therefore the Spartans are exceedingly wise. The premise that virtue is knowledge can thus lead to ridiculous results, for "virtue" is an ambiguous term, just as Protagoras has intimated: such courage as the Spartans possess (342b5) is not based on or identical to wisdom (compare 329e5–330a2, where Protagoras places wisdom and courage together). The long speech that follows will state some of the serious consequences of the view that "virtue is knowledge," i.e., something of what it would mean to possess such virtue as is properly identified with knowledge.

In his laconic way, Simonides contends that while it is in truth difficult to become good, it is impossible to be (to remain) good over time; and because it is impossible so to remain, Pittacus was wrong to assert that becoming noble is merely difficult. All human excellence is doomed to decline as a result of time, toil, and illness, for example (345b2–4), and it is precisely those who have gained the most knowledge and so act or fare best who have the most to lose—and will lose it eventually. Perhaps there is some consolation in the conviction that "best for the longest time are those whom the gods love" (345c3), but even this formulation suggests that the gods do not love all, that they do not protect forever those whom they do love, and that the goodness of the good does not owe its origin to the gods or their love. Simonides' poem, as interpreted by Socrates, insists on the frailty of human goodness and the necessarily exposed character of our happiness: knowledge or virtue is no guarantee against decline or misfortune. There is no "providential" care of human beings sufficient always to protect us.

Going together with this harsh view is an explicit statement of Socrates' own thought, the only one in a passage that otherwise presents itself as his explication of Simonides' intention: "I pretty much think that none of the wise men holds that any human being willingly [voluntarily] errs or willingly [voluntarily] carries out any shameful and bad deed. Rather, they well know that all who do the shameful and bad things do them unwillingly [involuntarily]" (345d9–e3). This view of the wise is but a variation on Socrates' dictum that virtue is knowledge and vice ignorance or (as he puts it in the *Protagoras*) that "this alone constitutes bad action, namely being deprived of knowledge" (345b5): all shameful and bad action is the product of a regrettable but—strictly speaking—involuntary ignorance (of the good), involuntary because no one would willingly or knowingly retain such ignorance; it is indeed contrary to "human nature" to seek out bad things when it is possible to secure the good (358d1–2). Thus the wise, who understand these things and their consequences, do not blame those who do any shameful or bad deed.

In the immediate context, this means that Simonides is not finally among the class of wise men, for he agrees with their defining opinion only partially or inconsistently: Simonides' last word here is "I blame" (347a3), and he blames Pittacus for the errors he makes because those errors concern "the greatest things" (347a2; compare 358c3–5 and context). (Simonides contends that he will not blame the middle or middling view, but Pittacus' is just that: Hesiod maintains that virtue is easy, Pittacus that it is difficult but possible to possess, Simonides that it is impossible to do so.) Could it be that Simonides' self-contradiction here, on this point, is not a prudent adaptation to political or familial authority but is rather the product of a certain confusion or that his attachment to justice goes well beyond the recognition of its utility to the city, of its necessity as (mere) convention (346c3–5)? We suggest that, as Protagoras began the section on poetry with an implicit message to Socrates, so Socrates concludes it with one to Protagoras: the sophist who is concerned with wisdom for the sake of honor or ambition (343b7–c3) and who seeks to gain a victory over a wise man (343a2) is not himself wise because he is inconsistent on a matter of fundamental importance. It is the burden of the remaining section of the dialogue to determine whether Protagoras shares some such inconsistency and, if he does, what its specific character is. In doing so, moreover, the final part of the dialogue also clarifies what the health of the soul would have to include according to Socrates and therewith a part of what the "physician of the soul" would look to in applying his treatments.

THE UNITY OF VIRTUE: COURAGE

After a brief interlude in which Protagoras appears to be shamed into continuing the conversation (348c1 and context), Socrates turns to examine the one virtue that Protagoras himself had introduced (329e5–6) but that they have yet to examine, courage. Protagoras is now willing to amend his earlier position by conceding that the four other virtues—wisdom, moderation, justice, and piety—are "reasonably comparable to one another" (349d2–4). On the one hand, this concession gives to Socrates a much clearer victory over Protagoras than did their original argument. On the other hand, by thus dropping the delicate question of the relation of wisdom to justice, Protagoras spares himself the threat of further embarrassment (or worse). Yet Protagoras does not concede everything to Socrates: courage, he insists, differs very much from the other virtues, for in the case of "many among the human beings," at least—surely not Protagoras himself! (compare 349d6 with 333c1–3 and context)—courage can go together with the greatest injustice, impiety, licentiousness, and lack of learning (ignorance). Courage, then, is not (necessarily) a "moral" virtue. It would seem to be rather a certain steadiness or toughness of soul, whether for the sake of heroic combat or illegal thievery.

Given this "amoral" view of courage, Socrates wonders what the relation of courage to mere boldness or confidence is. In his response, Protagoras now has recourse not to the many but to their opposite: the courageous are indeed bold; they are even eager in the face of things "the many" fear to advance toward. The crucial premise in the ensuing exchange is Protagoras' contention—perhaps made with a view to what he must claim publicly as a teacher of virtue, lest he be held to be "mad" (349e3–8; compare 323b2–7)—that the whole of virtue and hence courage in particular is altogether noble: the courageous are indeed bold, but not all the bold are courageous; only those who are bold in a noble way can be said to be courageous, and what distinguishes the noble virtue of courage from its shameful counterpart is knowledge. But why is knowledge so important? In the examples given—those of expert divers, cavalry men, and light-shieldsmen (peltasts)—knowledge has the effect of diminishing the risk to the courageous themselves or of thus benefiting them, and in this respect Protagoras' understanding of courage is consistent with his implicit account of justice: justice is service to the good of others and hence foolish or "shameful"; courage is the strength of soul needed to accomplish good things with a minimum of risk to oneself and hence is sensible or "noble." This amounts to saying that Protagoras does not here recognize any class of noble things that transcend the good or advantageous for oneself, that are choice worthy on account of their intrinsic worth or beauty regardless of whether they are advantageous to those who possess them or act in accord with them. Far from objecting to Socrates' account of courage that links its noble character to advantageous knowledge, Protagoras here accepts it.

Socrates attempts to take advantage of Protagoras' insistence that courage is marked by (a certain) knowledge, in contrast to his previous claim that courage can be combined with the greatest ignorance (compare 350a2–3 and a6–b1 with 349d4–8; 360e1–2), for this final step would allow Socrates to conclude, by means fair or foul, that virtue is knowledge. In response, Protagoras focuses on a logical blunder he attributes to Socrates, and because Socrates does not even attempt to defend himself, it could well appear that this first section (349a8–351b2) of the last part of the dialogue constitutes a victory for Protagoras. His selfish account of nobility is permitted to stand.

Protagoras' presentation of courage is not without complication. To repeat, Protagoras begins by insisting that great courage can go together with great ignorance, but he subsequently traces the noble character of courage, understood as a virtue, to precisely its being guided by knowledge; and then again, in response to Socrates' suggestion that "wisdom would be courage," Protagoras appears to separate courage from boldness entirely and to trace the source of boldness to (among other things) knowledge,[5] whereas courage he traces, not now to knowledge, but to nature and the proper rearing of souls. Protagoras, it seems, uses "courage" ambiguously, in both a political and a private sense: courage is that habituation, achieved through the training of the *body*, meant to ensure that citizens never act as cowards in war and hence in service to the city, as Protagoras had noted in his description of the political "education" (326b6–c3);[6] and it is that steadiness or toughness, the product of both nature and the proper training of the *soul* (351a5–b2), needed to benefit oneself in certain situations. It is true that neither conception of courage can be said to be knowledge, strictly speaking, but the latter is at least in service of knowledge: those who know the truth about justice and the gods, for example, must also be courageous enough to act on that knowledge or to live their lives in accord with it. Protagoras surely understands himself to possess some such

---

5. Consider 351a7 in the light of a2; on the kinship between *technē* and *epistēmē*, see 357b4.
6. This meaning of courage may shed light on why Protagoras identifies justice, moderation, and piety as being, in sum, "the virtue of a man [*anēr*]" (325a1–2): the *anēr*, the "real man," is distinguished by his spirited devotion to the common good and its supports. For a playful example of courage employed in the name of justice, see 310d3–4.

courage as this, for he enters large foreign cities to teach the young there, an act at once very risky, as he stresses, and very much to his advantage if successful (316c5–d3; *Meno* 91d2–4).

HEDONISM AND THE POWER OF KNOWLEDGE

Socrates suddenly shifts direction by taking up the question of whether pleasure is the good. He prompts Protagoras to agree that to live with distress and pain would not be to live well, but Protagoras does not agree that to live pleasantly is to live well: that is so, he suggests, only if one "should live his life by taking pleasures in the *noble* things" (*tois kalois g'*: 351c1–2). Protagoras, then, is no hedonist; at any rate he is unwilling to admit publicly that he is one (note the mention of what is "safer" in his response: 351d3). Whether sincere or calculated, his stated position compels him to recognize a distinction between noble and base pleasures, which is to say that he here recognizes nobility as a standard higher than pleasure. Now, if Protagoras is to be consistent with his just-stated view of the nobility of courage, he should mean by "noble things" no more than the good or advantageous: just as the nobility of courage stems from its knowledgeable use in order to benefit oneself under certain circumstances, so the nobility of the noble pleasures should stem from their being conducive to one's own good.

Evidently assuming such consistency on the part of Protagoras, Socrates immediately equates the noble things with the good and the shameful things with the bad, for he does not ask whether Protagoras calls some pleasant things *ignoble* and some painful things *noble*, as one might expect given Protagoras' statement, but rather whether he calls "some pleasant things *bad* and some distressing things *good*" (351c2–3, emphasis added). Protagoras refuses to state flatly that all pleasures are good or that pleasure itself is the good; he contends, rather, that there are some bad or harmful pleasures and some good or beneficial pains, a view characteristic of the many, according to Socrates: Protagoras and the many are united in their rejection of hedonism or in their shared conviction that only noble pleasures are good (consider also 352b2, where Socrates again attributes to him the view of the many on this score). Still, Protagoras, in contrast to the many, need not mean by "noble" here anything other than the (truly) advantageous.

The disagreement between Socrates and Protagoras concerning hedonism is momentarily abandoned when the two join forces to criticize the many for their view that it is not so much knowledge that rules us and determines our actions as it is the passions—spirited anger, pleasure, pain, erotic love, fear. Yet as Socrates explicitly indicates (351e3–352a1 and following), the purpose of investigating this latter question concerning knowledge is to make clear that pleasure is the good, i.e., to overturn the view that Protagoras appears to hold in common with the many. What then is the connection between hedonism and the stated view of the power of knowledge? We will be able to determine this connection only by first setting forth Socrates' arguments meant to establish that it is knowledge alone that determines our actions or that one who knows the good will of necessity pursue it.

Socrates first argues to the many that, whatever they may claim, they are hedonists in fact because they are unable to state any end of their actions other than the attainment of long-term pleasure or the avoidance of long-term pain (352e5–354e2). Indeed, Socrates asks repeatedly whether the many could state any other end that governs them (353c9–353e1; 354a3–c3; 354c3–e2; 355a1–5), on each occasion insisting that they could not. Second, according to Socrates, to be "overcome by oneself"—to give in to temptation, as we might say—is nothing other than to make a mistake in one's calculations concerning pleasure and pain; Socrates insists, in other words, that this failing is a purely intellectual one (354e3–356c3). Finally, Socrates proposes, as a remedy sufficient to correct this failing, a scientific "art of measuring" that would precisely determine the means to maximize pleasure and to minimize pain throughout life and so "save" or "preserve" it (356c4–357e8).

Two difficulties with Socrates' argument deserve mention. First, Socrates' purely intellectual account of weakness does not seem to fit the facts in every respect. Is it not the case that some human beings are by nature unable to withstand the pull of certain immediate pleasures, or the repulsive force of certain pains, whatever their intellect may tell them? Do not some *know* that it is better (or more productive of pleasure in the long run) to visit the doctor regularly than to fail to do so, for example, but are nonetheless unable to bring themselves to do it? Socrates here dismisses out of hand the possibility of such underlying weakness. Second, is it true that the many could not state an end of their actions, or at least of some of them, other than pleasure? For the experience of being overcome ("giving in to temptation") amounts to pursuing, for the sake of the advantage or pleasure involved, an action that appears both advantageous or pleasant *and* shameful, just as resisting temptation is to refuse to pursue such an action in order to be noble or to avoid shame. It is then the nobility of an action that is (also) of concern to us, that is the end of (some of) our actions—as both Protagoras and Socrates have already indicated (351c1–3). In persistently arguing that the many make mistakes merely in calculating their own long-term pleasure, rather than in weighing the pleasant or advantageous against what is noble, Socrates seems intent on stripping their view of its concern for nobility, of its "moral" character.[7]

We may now make a tentative suggestion as to a possible connection between hedonism, which Protagoras rejects, and the view that those who know the good necessarily seek it out, which he accepts. It is helpful to begin by returning to the view, stated by Socrates in his explication of the thought of Simonides in particular and "all" the wise in general, according to which being deprived of knowledge *alone* constitutes bad action or faring badly and hence (one may infer) acquiring or retaining knowledge *alone* constitutes good action or faring well (345b5 and context). The possession of knowledge, i.e., wisdom, is thus the proper end of human life, and this makes possible a clear calculus, an art of measuring, by which to live: all that contributes to this end is virtue, all that detracts from it vice. But as we have already noted, the wise also refuse to blame anyone for any shameful or bad deed; evidently they cannot discern in the world the necessary supports of what might be called moral desert. Moreover, Socrates also sketches in the same context a world without "providence": the good necessarily decline at the hands of illness, toil, and time, and neither gods nor knowledge protects them from these in the end. Such convictions of the wise, whatever their ultimate basis, would require of those who come to hold them considerable fortitude or toughness, a kind of courage (among of course other qualities). For if knowledge is indeed the good we seek, as the wise contend, there can be no guarantee that the world revealed by our seeking will support our hopes concerning it. If knowledge about the most important things comes at the price of our initial and perhaps dearest expectations of the world, it would to that extent be profoundly un-

---

7. Compare Socrates' initial statement of the many's view with his second: in the former, the difficulty is that they give in to things they know to be "base" or "low" or even "wicked" (*ponēra*), whereas in the latter it is that one gives in to things he knows to be "bad" (*kakos*), ultimately in the sense of unpleasant for oneself (compare 353c6–8 with 355a5–8). The first statement describes more accurately the phenomenon at issue.

pleasant or painful and hence would require some capacity in addition to a great intellect not only to grasp it but also to live in accord with it. Those who cannot endure such pain would then cling with greater tenacity to opinions that act as a salve for it or prophylactic against it, opinions of the kind that Socrates obscures or abstracts from in his presentation of the many. And so—to return now to the question of hedonism in its relation to the power of knowledge—the toughness indicated would be unnecessary only if pleasure is *the* good and knowledge or wisdom is a pleasure untainted by pain: no particular toughness would be required to seek out, attain, and act in accord with knowledge so understood because it would be by definition pleasing to us.

The purpose of these complex passages is not to establish the truth of hedonism, a doctrine Socrates elsewhere criticizes. Indeed, Socrates proves at most that the opinions of the many are confused: on the one hand they deny that pleasure is the good (351c3), deferring instead to what is noble; on the other hand they assert that pleasure is the good.[8] The purpose of these passages is rather to make clear that, his manifest contempt for them notwithstanding (317a4–5; 352e3–4; 353a7–8), Protagoras is as confused as the many; we understand now why Socrates had indicated in this context that he was about to reveal a further aspect of Protagoras' thought (352a8–b1). Protagoras should maintain that the good is pleasure, if he wishes to maintain also that knowledge alone is sufficient to guide us aright. That he resists hedonism may mean in the context that he is insufficiently aware of the cost we may incur in pursuing the good that is wisdom or understanding, for he in effect assumes that the good has the character of the pleasant, which requires no special fortitude to pursue, even as he refuses to profess to being a hedonist. Put another way, Protagoras underestimates the importance of, and himself may lack, the steadiness or toughness needed in every case to follow the dictates of knowledge. And because he does not abandon his lofty view of knowledge (352c8–d3), he is compelled in the sequel to accept or at least relent to a version of hedonism. This proves to be an element of his undoing.

---

8. One may wonder whether he does even that much: although Socrates begins from the premise that all pleasures are good—a premise compatible with the view that the good includes other things in addition to pleasure—he adopts the premise, in his cross-examination of the many, that the good is pleasure (and only pleasure); compare 351c4–d2 and 358a5–6 with 355a1–5.

THE REFUTATION OF PROTAGORAS: COURAGE AS KNOWLEDGE

Socrates prepares to examine Protagoras by first opening up the conversation to include the others present (358a1–359a1; compare 314b7–8), and he establishes the following theses, with the aid of all or most of those present (compare *sunedokei* at 358b6 with the more inclusive agreements at 358b2–3, c6, d4, and 359a1; Socrates makes explicit his own agreement only at 358d4): all actions conducive to living pleasantly and free of pain are noble, and a noble deed is as such both good and advantageous. Moreover, only ignorance, or having a false opinion about the most important things, is responsible for our errors in choosing better from worse, since no one willingly advances toward or does things he supposes to be bad—no one, that is, who either knows or supposes that other things are better than those that he does, then does the inferior things. And since being afraid of something is to expect something bad or harmful from it, no one willingly advances toward that which he is afraid of, if it is possible not to do so.

Socrates now trains his sights on Protagoras (359a2 and following). Since it has just been shown to be impossible, given human nature, for human beings to advance willingly toward things they are frightened of, the courageous as much as the cowards must advance toward things they are confident (bold) about, that is, toward things from which they expect to gain some benefit: the courageous man enters battle because he believes doing so to be noble, hence good—hence pleasant (360a1–3)! In this way Socrates does everything in his power to link courage with knowledge or wisdom—the knowledge of what is advantageous for oneself—and so to strip courage of that which most elicits our admiration of it, its noble (self-sacrificing) character. That the good is here identified with the pleasant only furthers this goal, for the pleasure-seeking courageous differ from the pleasure-seeking cowards merely in their divergent opinions as to what is good and hence pleasant. Courage is now nothing other than knowledge of what is truly frightening or terrible, cowardice the ignorance of it. And this means either that the courageous will enter battle because they know there to be nothing truly frightening in doing so—and hence there to be nothing truly heroic in so acting, as with the highly skilled divers, cavalrymen, and light-shieldsmen earlier—or that the courageous will know that it is indeed frightening to enter battle and so will do the only sensible thing in the face of such harmful terrors: flee them. It is these consequences of the proposition that virtue is knowledge, or more precisely of the reduction of courage to knowledge, that Protagoras cannot finally stomach, for he too is moved by the willingness of the courageous to enter battle, come what may for themselves (359e1–4).

What Protagoras seeks to exploit in the case of justice, then, he admires in the case of courage, namely the willingness to sacrifice oneself for the sake of a good other and greater than one's own. Protagoras too, it turns out, admires a nobility not reducible to one's own good, to say nothing of one's own pleasure. This admiration is in harmony with the sensitivity to shame he has exhibited in the dialogue, especially such sensitivity as prompts him to continue a conversation the progress of which he surely, and rightly, suspects will harm him (348c1; consider also 333c1). And earlier in the conversation (332c3–6), Socrates had unobtrusively brought out Protagoras' conviction, as further evidence of a general conclusion that had already been established clearly enough (332c1–3), that there is only one contrary of the noble (namely the shameful) and only one of the good (namely the bad). But to agree to this is to hold that the noble and the good are distinct from one another, not that the noble is reducible to the good as Protagoras had maintained in his first discussion of courage. And although the separation of the noble from the good may have a nasty implication, to the effect that nobility is bad ("it is bad to be noble"), it may also mean that nobility is *higher* than any merely personal good and hence amounts to one vital aspect of the moral view: morality seems to demand that we sometimes choose to do what is noble whether or not we benefit ourselves thereby. To summarize, Protagoras had recourse in his initial discussion of courage to a nobility reducible to the good for oneself, and he subsequently reaffirms his view that "all noble actions" are as such "good" (359e5–8); but Protagoras has shown himself to be unable to stick to this view of nobility because he has shown himself to believe that some things are noble and hence choice worthy despite the fact that—or precisely if—they are bad or disadvantageous for oneself. Protagoras has thus shown himself to be confused.

Conclusion

Toward the end of the *Protagoras*, Socrates notes that a strange inversion has taken place. For whereas Socrates had begun his examination of Protagoras by stating that he himself did not hold virtue to be teachable, he notes now that he has been arguing that virtue is knowledge and therefore teachable; and just as Protagoras had begun by contending that virtue is indeed teachable, so now at the end of the conversation he resists Socrates' attempt to link courage with knowledge and hence to imply, at least, its teachable character (361a3–d6). To account for this peculiarity, one must track the different meanings of "virtue" in the dialogue: "virtue" first comes to sight as justice, piety, and moderation—all virtues conducive to political life and instilled in us by nursemaid, mother, father, teachers, and, as their ultimate guide, the laws themselves. What Protagoras offers his students instead is indicated by his unexpected expansion of virtue to include courage and wisdom, wisdom being the greatest of the virtues. According to Protagoras, moral or political virtue can be beaten into one but it cannot be taught, strictly speaking, whereas courage and wisdom can be taught because they are rational or consist in knowledge, in the knowledge of the priority of the good for oneself (or the foolish character of justice) together with the necessary strength of soul both to see through the conventional virtues and to act accordingly. Protagoras thus admires those who, through the right combination of toughness and understanding, seek and attain their own good in the face of what family, friends, city, and gods say. But, as we have seen, he himself lacks such a combination of qualities; his knowledge of what is good does not consistently determine his actions because he lacks the "courage of his convictions." In particular, he cannot consistently stick to the reduction of the noble to the good that the admiration indicated implies; or, he admires also those who are willing to sacrifice themselves, if not in the name of justice then in the name of courage. And being confused on this point, he could hardly bring his students to clarity concerning it.

One might say that the *Protagoras* both diminishes the differences between philosopher and sophist (314d3) and sharpens those that remain: like Protagoras, Socrates holds the initial education we receive not to be an education properly speaking (pp. 72–73), for his denial of the teachability of virtue pertains only to "the political art" and to political virtue strictly construed, not to virtue understood as knowledge (of the good). The chief difference between the two comes to sight when one considers Socrates' failed attempt to persuade Protagoras of the unity of the virtues as aspects of knowledge, a proposition to which Protagoras relents rather than agrees (360d8–e5). The subordination of the virtues (or most of them)[9] to knowledge seems to bring with it the consequence to which Protagoras objects so

9. Consider 361b1–3, noting especially *panta* ("all") at 361b1 and the incomplete list that follows.

strongly (see also *Meno* 87e5–89a5 for a comparable reaction). In order to agree to it, then, one would have to be free of the confusion characteristic of (even) Protagoras, who (to repeat) understands himself to seek only his own advantage but in fact also admires those who sacrifice theirs. Socrates is surely free of this confusion. But because a full account of the consequences of this freedom goes beyond the present reading of the *Protagoras*, it must suffice to conclude by noting that, in reporting his conversation with Protagoras, Socrates permits us to put ourselves to the same tests to which he subjects Protagoras and so to begin to understand our own concern for virtue—a service that, being carried out without expectation of payment, makes clear Socrates' relative indifference to lucre and the generosity that is compatible with the pursuit of true virtue.

Meno
(Or, On Virtue)[1]

DRAMATIS PERSONAE: MENO, SOCRATES, A SLAVE OF MENO'S, ANYTUS

70a   MENO: Can you tell me, Socrates, whether virtue is something teachable? Or whether it isn't something teachable but is rather something that can be acquired by practice? Or whether it isn't something that can be acquired by practice or learning, but is present in human beings[2] by nature or in some other way?

SOCRATES: Meno[3], previously Thessalians[4] were well thought of

---

1. It is uncertain whether the subtitles accompanying the dialogues are Plato's own or were added later, perhaps by the Hellenistic critic Thrasylus (see Diogenes Laertius 3.56–62). For the case that the subtitles date from the fourth century B.C., and may well be Plato's own, see R. G. Hoerber, "Thrasylus' Platonic Canon and the Double Titles," *Phronesis* 2:10–20.
2. *Anthrōpoi*. The word can simply designate the human race (as distinguished from animals or gods, for example) but also can be a term of disparagement: better to be a real man (*anēr*) or gentleman (*kaloskagathos*) than a mere *anthrōpos*. It will be translated as "human being" ("human beings"), "person" ("people"), or "fellow."
3. Meno was of a prominent family in Pharsalus in the region of Thessaly. He was 18 or 19 years old when the dialogue probably takes place (402 B.C.) and may have been staying with his "ancestral guest-friend" Anytus on official business: the victory of Lycophron of Pherae over Larissa prompted the Aleuadae and the ruling house of Pharsalus to seek Athenian assistance; see R. S. Bluck, *Plato's Meno* (Cambridge: Cambridge University Press, 1964), 123 n. 3, and on 90b5.
4. Thessaly was a region north of Athens that included the principal city of Larissa mentioned in the next sentence. The Thessalians were indeed renowned for their horsemanship (see *Hippias Major* 284a and *Laws* 625d), but Socrates' remarks concerning their love of wisdom are "doubtless a piece of veiled irony" (Bluck ad loc.). In the *Crito*, Socrates has the Laws say that there is in Thessaly "the greatest disorder and licentiousness" (53d2–4).

91

among the Greeks and admired for both their horsemanship and
their wealth. But now, in my opinion, they are so also for their wis-
70b   dom, and above all the Larissaeans, the fellow citizens of your comrade Aristippus.[5] Gorgias[6] is responsible[7] for this for you:[8] when he
came to the city he took as lovers of his wisdom the first men of both
the Aleuadae[9]—among whom is your lover Aristippus—and the rest
of the Thessalians. In particular, he has made it a customary habit for
you[10] to answer in a fearless and magnificent[11] manner if someone
asks something, as is fitting for those who know, since he too makes
70c   himself available to any Greek who wants to ask whatever he wants,
and there isn't anyone he doesn't answer.[12]

But here, dear Meno, the contrary has come to pass. It is as if there's
been a sort of drought in wisdom, and it's likely that wisdom has left
71a   these locales for yours. At any rate, if you're willing to ask someone
here in this way, there isn't anyone who won't laugh and say:
"Stranger, it's likely that in your opinion I'm a blessed sort of person—to know, that is, whether virtue is something teachable or in
what way it comes to be present. But I'm so far from knowing
whether it is something teachable or isn't something teachable that I
don't even happen to know at all what in the world virtue itself is."
71b   Now I myself, Meno, am in this condition too. I share the poverty
of my fellow citizens in this matter,[13] and I reproach myself on the
grounds that I don't know about virtue at all. And as for that about
which I don't know *what* it is, how would I know what *sort* of a thing
it is? Or is it possible in your opinion for anyone who doesn't know

5. Aristippus became involved in Cyrus' attempt to overthrow his brother, Artaxerxes II, in
401 B.C.; see Xenophon, *Anabasis of Cyrus* 1.1.10, 1.2.1. Xenophon tells us also that Meno received from Aristippus the command of mercenary troops while "still in the bloom of his
youth" (*Anabasis* 2.6.28).
6. Gorgias of Leontini was one of the most famous rhetoricians or sophists in antiquity. His
visit to Athens is recorded by Plato in the dialogue named after him.
7. *Aitia*: the word has a range of meanings, from (natural) cause to (moral) responsibility or
blame.
8. The plural "you."
9. The ruling family or clan in Larissa. The Aleuadae had supported the Persians in their
invasion of Greece in 480 B.C. (see Herodotus 9.1).
10. The plural "you."
11. Literally, "in a manner befitting greatness" (*megaloprepōs*). The adverb appears also at
94b, the noun at 74a and 88a.
12. For an example, see *Gorgias* 447d–448a.
13. The word (*pragma*) has a range of meanings, from "matter" or "affair" to "thing," in the
sense of a concrete reality, to "thing of consequence" or that which is an object of concern
or trouble.

at all who Meno is to know whether he is beautiful[14] or wealthy or again wellborn, or the contraries of these? Is it possible in your opinion?

MENO: Not in mine, at least. But Socrates, do you truly not know even 71c what virtue is, and are we in addition to report these things about you back home?

SOCRATES: Not only that, comrade, but also that I've never yet met up with another who does know, in my opinion.

MENO: What's that? Didn't you meet up with Gorgias when he was here?

SOCRATES: I did indeed.

MENO: Well, then, wasn't it your opinion that he knew?

SOCRATES: I don't have a very good memory, Meno, so I'm not able to say at present what my opinion of him was then. But perhaps he does know, and you [know] what he said. So recollect for me how he 71d spoke. And if you like, you yourself say, for doubtless you share his opinions.

MENO: I do indeed.

SOCRATES: Then let's let him be, since he is in fact absent. But you yourself, Meno, in the name of the gods, what do you assert virtue to be? Say and don't be begrudging, so I may have uttered a most fortunate falsehood[15] if you and Gorgias manifestly come to sight as knowing, whereas I said that I'd never yet met up with anyone who knows.

71e MENO: But it isn't difficult to say, Socrates. In the first place, if you want the virtue of a man, that's easy. This is the virtue of a man: to be capable of carrying out the affairs of the city and, in doing so, to benefit friends, harm enemies, and take care that he himself not suffer any such thing. And if you want the virtue of a woman, it isn't difficult to define: she must manage the household well by both preserving its contents and being obedient to the man.[16] And there is one virtue of a child, both female and male, and another of an older man, 72a whether free or, if you like, slave. There are also very many other virtues, so there's no perplexity in speaking about what virtue is. For

14. *Kalos*: the word may denote both physical and moral beauty; it and only it will be translated as "noble" ("nobly") or "beautiful" ("beautifully").

15. Or, "lie" (*pseusma*).

16. The word for "woman" in Greek can also mean "wife," just as the word for "man" can also mean "husband."

the virtue belonging to each of us is related to each task appropriate to each action and time of life. I think it is similar, Socrates, for vice as well.

SOCRATES: I seem to have availed myself of a certain great good fortune, Meno, if in seeking[17] one virtue I have discovered a kind of beehive[18] of virtues with you. But Meno, in accord with this image of the

72b   beehives, if upon my asking you what in the world the being of a bee is, you were to say that they are many and varied, what would you answer me if I asked you: "Do you assert that they are many and varied and differ from one another in this respect, in their being bees? Or do they not differ at all in this, but in some other respect—for example, in beauty or size or some other such thing?" Tell me, what would you answer if you were asked in this way?

MENO: For my part, this: they don't differ at all in being bees, the one from the other.

72c   SOCRATES: If, then, I said next: "Well, tell me this very thing, Meno. What do you assert that is with respect to which they do not differ at all but are all the same?" Doubtless you'd be able to say something to me?

MENO: I would indeed.

SOCRATES: Then do so also concerning the virtues. Even if they are many and varied, do they all have some one form[19] that is the same, on account of which they are virtues and to which, I suppose, the person answering would nobly look in making clear to his questioner

72d   what virtue is? Or don't you understand what I mean?

MENO: In my opinion, at least, I do understand. But I don't yet grasp the question the way I want to.

SOCRATES: Is it this way in your opinion only concerning virtue, Meno—that there is one for a man, another for a woman and the rest—or is it similar as regards health too, and size and strength? Is there in your opinion one health for a man, but another for a woman? Or, if in fact there is health, does it have the same form everywhere,

72e   whether in a man or in anyone else whatever?

MENO: The health, at least, of both a man and a woman is the same in my opinion.

---

17. Sometimes also translated as "search for" or "inquire into" (*zēteō*).
18. Or, "swarm" (*smēnos*).
19. The first mention in the dialogue of the famous Socratic "forms" (*eidē*), the primary meaning of which is simply the outward look or appearance of a thing.

SOCRATES: Then also size and strength? If in fact a woman is strong, will she be strong by virtue of the same form and the same strength? For I mean by "the same," this: strength doesn't differ at all in regard to its being strength, whether it be in a man or in a woman. Or is there any difference in your opinion?

MENO: Not in mine, at least.

73a SOCRATES: Will virtue differ at all in its being virtue, whether it be in a child or in an elder, whether in a woman or in a man?

MENO: In my opinion, at least, Socrates, this is somehow no longer similar to those others.

SOCRATES: What's that? Weren't you saying that the virtue of a man is to manage a city well, that of a woman a household?

MENO: I was indeed.

73b SOCRATES: Then is it possible to manage well either a city or a household, or anything else whatever, for one who doesn't do so moderately and justly?

MENO: No indeed.

SOCRATES: Then if in fact they manage justly and moderately, they will do so by means of justice and moderation?

MENO: Necessarily.

SOCRATES: Both require the same things, then, if in fact they are to be good, both the woman and the man, namely justice and moderation.

MENO: They appear to.

SOCRATES: What then? Could a child and an elder ever become good by being licentious and unjust?

MENO: No indeed.

SOCRATES: But [by being] moderate and just?

MENO: Yes.

73c SOCRATES: All human beings, then, are good in the same way, for by attaining the same things they become good.

MENO: It's likely.

SOCRATES: Doubtless, then, they would not be good in the same way if their virtue were not the same.

MENO: No indeed.

SOCRATES: Well, then, since the virtue of all is the same, try to say and to recall what Gorgias asserts it to be, and you following him.

MENO: What else than to be able to rule human beings? If in fact you
73d are seeking some one thing that pertains to all.

SOCRATES: But that *is* what I'm seeking. But is the virtue of a child and a slave the same, Meno—for both to be able to rule the master—and is it your opinion that one who rules would still be a slave?[20]

MENO: That's really not so, in my opinion, Socrates.

SOCRATES: Because it isn't likely, best one. For[21] examine, in addition, the following. You assert, "to be able to rule." Won't we add to this, "justly, but not unjustly"?

MENO: For my part, I think so: justice, Socrates, *is* virtue.

73e   SOCRATES: Is it virtue, Meno, or a certain virtue?

MENO: How do you mean that?

SOCRATES: As with anything else whatever. Take, for example, roundness, if you like. For my part I would say that it is a certain shape, not so simply that it is shape. And I would speak in this way on account of there being other shapes as well.

MENO: You'd do so correctly, since I too say that justice is not the only virtue but that there are others as well.

74a   SOCRATES: What are these? State them. For example, I would say to you the other shapes, if you should bid me to do so. So you too state for me other virtues.

MENO: Well, courage is a virtue, in my opinion at least, and moderation and wisdom and magnificence and very many others.

SOCRATES: Once again, Meno, we have suffered the same thing. Though we seek only one, we have again discovered many virtues, if in a manner different than just now. But as for the one virtue which is present throughout all these, we aren't able to discover it.

MENO: For I'm not yet able, Socrates, in the way that you are seeking
74b   it, to get hold of the one virtue pertaining to all, as with the other things.

SOCRATES: That's likely, at least. But I'll be eager, if I can, to push us forward.[22] For you understand, I suppose, that it is this way with everything. If someone should ask you what I was saying just now: "What is shape, Meno?"—if you were to say to him "roundness," and if he said to you what in fact I did, "Is roundness shape or a certain shape?"—doubtless you would say that it is a certain shape.

20. There is some disagreement among the mss. The emendation of the text adopted by Bluck would read: "But is the virtue of a child the same [i.e., to be able to rule human beings], Meno, and is the virtue of a slave to be able to rule the master?"

21. The word translated "for" (*gar*) is excised by some editors but is present in the mss.

22. Reading *probibasai* with Croiset, Burnet, and two of the mss.; the reading adopted, with some mss. support, by Bluck and Sharples (*prosbibasai*) would translate as: "I'll be eager, if I can, for us to advance."

MENO: Certainly.

74c   SOCRATES: On account of this, that there are also other shapes?

MENO: Yes.

SOCRATES: And if he asked you in addition what sort they are, you would tell him?

MENO: I would indeed.

SOCRATES: And if in turn he asked you in a similar way about what color is, and when you said white, the questioner then replied, "Is white color or a certain color?" would you say that it is a certain color, because there happen to be other ones as well?

MENO: I would indeed.

SOCRATES: And if he bade you to state the other colors, you would say
74d   them, which happen to be colors no less than white is?

MENO: Yes.

SOCRATES: If, then, he pursued the argument[23] as I was and said, "We always arrive at many things, but don't [answer] me in this way. Instead, since you address by some one name these many things, and you assert that none of them is not shape even though these are contraries of one another, what is this which holds fast the round no less than the straight, which you name 'shape,' so that you assert that the round is
74e   no more shape than the straight?" Or don't you speak in this way?

MENO: I do indeed.

SOCRATES: When you speak in this way, then, do you assert that the round is no more round than straight and that the straight is no more straight than round?

MENO: No, doubtless, Socrates.

SOCRATES: But surely you assert that the round is no more shape than the straight and that the latter is no more so than the former?

MENO: What you say is true.

SOCRATES: What in the world, then, is this, the name of which is
75a   "shape"? Try to say it. [MENO *fails to answer.*] Well, if you had said to the person asking in this way about either shape or color, "But for my part I don't even understand what you want, my fellow, for I don't know what you mean"—perhaps he would have wondered at this and said: "Don't you understand that I am seeking that which is the same in all these?"

---

23. *Logos*: this important term will be translated as "speech," "argument," or "account," depending on the context.

Or wouldn't you be able to say, in the case of these things, Meno, if someone should ask you, "What is this same thing that pertains to all, to the round and straight and all the other things that you do indeed call 'shapes'?" Try to say, so that you may become practiced with a view to answering about virtue.

75b   MENO: No, but *you* say, Socrates.

SOCRATES: Do you want me to gratify you?

MENO: Certainly.

SOCRATES: Will you too be willing, then, to speak to me about virtue?

MENO: I will indeed.

SOCRATES: Then I've got to be eager to do so, for that would be worthwhile.

MENO: Certainly.

SOCRATES: Come, then, let's try to say for you what shape is. Just examine whether you accept that it is the following. Let this be shape for us: that which alone of the beings happens always to accompany color. Is this adequate for you, or are you seeking it in some other way? For I would be content if you should speak to me about virtue
75c   in this way.

MENO: But that is naïve,[24] Socrates!

SOCRATES: How do you mean?

MENO: That shape is somehow, according to your account, that which always accompanies color.[25] Well, if someone should deny knowing color but is as perplexed about it as he is about shape, what answer do you suppose would have been given by you?

SOCRATES: For my part, what's true. And if the questioner should be one of the wise, as well as eristic[26] and contentious, I would say to
75d   him: "I've had my say. If I speak incorrectly, it's your task to receive the argument[27] and refute it." But if, being friends—just as you and I are now—they should want to converse[28] with one another, they

24. Or, "silly," "foolish" (*euēthes*).
25. Meno replaces the word Socrates had used for color (*chrōma*) with *chroa*, the first meaning of which is "skin," hence (superficial) "appearance," hence also "color." Socrates himself uses this word at 76d. See Jacob Klein, A *Commentary on Plato's Meno* (Chicago: University of Chicago Press, 1989 [1965]), 60–62, and Sharples ad loc.
26. That is, quarrelsome or disputatious.
27. This is half of the common phrase "to give and receive a *logos*": see, e.g., *Protagoras* 336c and 348a.
28. The verb (*dialegesthai*) is related to the adverb translated in the immediately following as "more dialectical" (*dialektikōteron*).

ought to answer in a way that is somehow gentler and more dialectical. And perhaps the more dialectical way is not only to answer
what's true but to do so also by means of those things the person being asked[29] agrees he knows. I too will try to speak to you in this way.

75e   So tell me. Do you call something an "end"? Such a sort of thing, I
mean, as a limit and extremity—by all these I mean the same thing.
Perhaps Prodicus[30] might differ with us, but you, at least, I suppose,
call something "limited" and "ended." It's this sort of thing I mean
to say, nothing complicated.

MENO: But I do call things this, and I think I understand what you
mean.

76a   SOCRATES: What, then? Do you call something a plane and another in
turn a solid—as, for example, those things in matters of geometry?

MENO: I do indeed so call things.

SOCRATES: Well, you might already understand from me, on the basis
of these things, what I say shape is. For with respect to every shape,
I say this: that which limits the solid is shape. Summing this up, I
would say that shape is the limit of a solid.

MENO: What do you say color is, Socrates?

SOCRATES: You are hubristic,[31] Meno! You burden an older man with
the trouble of answering, but you yourself are unwilling to recall and
76b   to say whatever in the world Gorgias says virtue is!

MENO: But when you tell me this, Socrates, I will tell you.

SOCRATES: Even someone who's been blindfolded would know,
Meno, when you converse with him, that you are beautiful and still
have lovers.

MENO: Why so?

SOCRATES: Because you do nothing but issue commands in the
speeches, which is what in fact the spoiled do, inasmuch as they are
76c   tyrants while they are in their bloom. And at the same time you've
perhaps detected my weakness when it comes to those who are beautiful. So I'll gratify you and answer.

MENO: Certainly, do gratify me.

SOCRATES: Do you want me to answer you, then, in the manner of
Gorgias—the way in which you would follow most of all?

29. Some editors read, with the Latin of Ficinus, "the person posing the questions."
30. A sophist from Ceos famous for his precise definitions of words; see, e.g., *Protagoras*
315d, 337a–338b, 341a–d.
31. Or, "arrogant."

MENO: I do want you to, of course.

SOCRATES: Do you[32] say, then, that there are certain effluences of the beings, in the manner of Empedocles?[33]

MENO: Absolutely.

SOCRATES: And that there are pores into which and through which the effluences proceed?

MENO: Certainly.

76d SOCRATES: And that some of the effluences fit into certain of the pores, but the others are too small or too large?

MENO: That is so.

SOCRATES: Then do you call something "sight" as well?

MENO: I do indeed.

SOCRATES: So on the basis of these things, "comprehend what I say to you," Pindar[34] said: color is an emanation of shapes[35] commensurate with sight and hence subject to perception.

MENO: In my opinion, Socrates, this is the best answer you've given.

SOCRATES: For perhaps it was spoken in accord with your customary way.[36] And at the same time, I think, you're reflecting on the fact that you might also say, on the basis of it, what sound is, as well as smell

76e and many other such things.

MENO: Certainly.

SOCRATES: For it is a tragic[37] answer, Meno. As a result, it's more satisfactory to you than the one concerning shape.

MENO: It is to me, at least.

SOCRATES: But it isn't better, son of Alexidemos, as I am persuaded, but that other one is. And I think you wouldn't be of the opinion that it is either, if it weren't necessary for you, as you were saying yesterday, to depart prior to the Mysteries[38] but could stay and be initiated.

---

32. The plural "you." One ms. reads: "Is it said that" (*legetai*).

33. Among the most famous of the "pre-Socratic" philosophers, Empedocles is thought to have been a teacher of Gorgias (see also *Theaetetus* 152e).

34. A leading lyric poet (518–438 B.C.). The poem from which this line is taken does not survive; see also Aristophanes, *Birds* 945, where the line is quoted, and Klein, 68 n. 40.

35. Or, "bodies," "figures." Socrates uses in his definition of color the same word (*schēma*) translated as "shape."

36. The phrase "customary way" here translates a word (*sunētheia*) that suggests customs or habits derived from dwelling or living together (*sunēthēs*); it appears nowhere else in Plato. ("Customary habit" translates *ethos* at 70b and 82a.)

37. Or, perhaps, "high-flown" (*tragikē*).

38. The word translated by "initiated" is related to the word for the Mysteries, the most solemn and august of the religious ceremonies.

77a   MENO: But I would stay, Socrates, if you were to say to me many things of this sort.

SOCRATES: Well, I'll lack nothing in point of eagerness, at any rate, both for your sake and my own, in saying such things. Yet I'm afraid I won't be able to say many things of this sort.

But come now, you too try to keep your promise to me by speaking about what virtue is as a whole, and stop making many out of the one, as the wits say every time people shatter something. Rather, leave virtue whole and sound and say what it is—you've got exam-
77b   ples from me.

MENO: Well, in my opinion, Socrates, virtue is, just as the poet says, "to rejoice in noble things and to be capable."[39] I too say that this is virtue: for one who desires the noble things to be capable of providing them for himself.

SOCRATES: Do you say that the one who desires the noble things is a desirer of goods?

MENO: Definitely.

SOCRATES: On the grounds that there are some who desire the bad
77c   things but others the good things? Don't all, best one, desire the good things, in your opinion?

MENO: Not in mine, at least.

SOCRATES: But some desire the bad things?

MENO: Yes.

SOCRATES: Supposing that the bad things are good, do you mean, or even knowing that they are bad they nonetheless desire them?

MENO: In my opinion, at least, they do both.

SOCRATES: In your opinion, Meno, is there anyone who knows that the bad things are bad and nonetheless desires them?

MENO: Definitely.

SOCRATES: What do you say that he desires? To possess them for him-self?

MENO: Yes, to possess them for himself—what else?

77d   SOCRATES: In the belief that the bad things benefit him who comes to possess them, or knowing that the bad things harm him to whom they are present?

MENO: There are some who believe the bad things benefit, and there are also others who know that they harm.

---

39. Or, "powerful." The source of this line is unknown.

SOCRATES: And in your opinion, do those who believe the bad things benefit know that the bad things are bad?

MENO: That's not at all the case, in my opinion at any rate.

SOCRATES: So it's clear, then, that these are not the ones who desire the
77e   bad things—those who are ignorant of them—but they desire rather those things they supposed to be good and are in fact bad. As a result, those who are ignorant of them and suppose them to be good clearly desire the good things. Or not?

MENO: They likely do, at least.

SOCRATES: What then? Those who desire the bad things, as you assert, and who believe the bad things harm him who possesses them— doubtless they know that they will be harmed by them?

MENO: Necessarily.

78a   SOCRATES: But don't they suppose that those who are harmed are wretched insofar as they are harmed?

MENO: This too is necessary.

SOCRATES: And that the wretched are unhappy?

MENO: I think so, for my part.

SOCRATES: So is there anyone who wants to be wretched and un-happy?

MENO: Not in my opinion, Socrates.

SOCRATES: Then no one, Meno, wants the bad things, unless he in fact wants to be such. For what is it to be wretched other than both to de-sire and to possess the bad things?

78b   MENO: It's likely that what you say is true, Socrates, and that no one wants the bad things.

SOCRATES: Weren't you saying just now that virtue is to want the good things and to be capable?

MENO: I did say that.

SOCRATES: Then although this is what was said,[40] the wanting is pres-ent in all, and in this respect at least, no one is any better than an-other?

MENO: It appears so.

SOCRATES: But it's clear that if in fact one is better than another, he would be better with respect to the "being capable."

MENO: Certainly.

---

40. Reading *toutou* with the mss., defended by Sharples, rather than Ast's conjecture *tou* adopted by most modern editors. The latter might be translated: "Then in what was said, the wanting is present."

SOCRATES: This, then, as is likely, is virtue according to your account:
78c   the capacity to provide the good things for oneself.

MENO: In my opinion, Socrates, it is altogether as you are now taking it to be.

SOCRATES: So let's see if this too that you are saying is true, for perhaps what you say might be good. Do you assert that virtue is being able to provide the good things for oneself?

MENO: I do indeed.

SOCRATES: And don't you call both health and wealth, for example, good?

MENO: I say possessing gold and silver is too, as well as honors in a city and offices.

SOCRATES: Don't you say that certain things other than those of that sort are good?

MENO: No, but I mean all things of that sort.

78d   SOCRATES: Well, then. Virtue is providing oneself with gold and silver, as Meno, the ancestral guest-friend[41] of the Great King,[42] asserts. Do you set down as an addition to this provision, Meno, "justly and piously," or does it make no difference to you? If someone provides himself with these things unjustly, do you call it "virtue" all the same?

MENO: Doubtless no, Socrates.

SOCRATES: But "vice"?

MENO: Certainly, doubtless.

SOCRATES: One ought, then, as is likely, to set down in addition to this
78e   providing, justice or moderation or piety, or some other part of virtue. Otherwise it won't be virtue, even though it does provide the good things.

MENO: For how, without these things, could it be virtue?

SOCRATES: Not providing gold and silver, either for oneself or for another, when providing it is unjust—isn't this very lack of provision[43] virtue?

MENO: It appears so.

SOCRATES: So the provision of such goods would no more be virtue

41. *Xenos*: the word may mean simply "stranger," but because there existed formal duties of mutual reciprocity among certain families of different cities (*xenia*), the "foreigner" may also be one's "guest-friend" to whom one owes hospitality (see also n. 84).
42. That is, the king of Persia.
43. Elsewhere translated as "perplexity" (*aporia*); the word can also mean "poverty" or "want" and thus plays on Meno's interest in wealth.

than not providing them. Instead, as is likely, what comes into being with justice will be virtue and what without all such sorts of things, vice.

79a   MENO: In my opinion, it is necessarily as you say.

SOCRATES: Did we assert a little before that each of these is a part of virtue, justice and moderation and all such things?

MENO: Yes.

SOCRATES: Well, then, Meno, are you playing with me?

MENO: Why, Socrates?

SOCRATES: Because when I just now asked you not to break up or to fragment virtue and gave you examples in accord with which you should answer, you neglected this, and you say to me that virtue is
79b   being able to provide the good things for oneself, together with justice. Do you assert that this is a part of virtue?

MENO: I do indeed.

SOCRATES: So it results from the things you agree to that doing whatever one does with a part of virtue is virtue. For you assert that justice is a part of virtue, as is each of these.

Why then do I say this? Because, though I asked you to speak about virtue as a whole, you are far from saying what it itself is but assert that every action is virtue if in fact it is done with a part of virtue—
79c   as though you had said what virtue as a whole is and as though by now I'd recognize it even if you break it up into parts. So don't you have need of the same question once again from the beginning, as seems to be the case to me, dear Meno? What is virtue, if [it should be true that]⁴⁴ every action accompanied by a part of virtue would be virtue? For that is what somebody is saying whenever he says that every action accompanied by justice is virtue. Or isn't it your opinion that the same question is needed once again, but do you suppose instead that someone knows what a part of virtue is, when he doesn't know it itself?

MENO: No, not in my opinion, at least.

79d   SOCRATES: For if you remember, when I replied to you just now about shape, we were rejecting, I think, the sort of answer that attempts to answer by means of things that are still being sought out and that have not yet been agreed to.

MENO: And we were rejecting it correctly, Socrates.

44. The grammar of the sentence presupposes the protasis of another, unstated condition.

SOCRATES: Well, then, best one, you too shouldn't suppose that when what virtue as a whole is is still being sought out, you'll make clear what it is to anyone at all by answering in terms of its parts, nor that you'll make clear anything else by speaking in this same way. Sup-

79e   pose instead that the same question will be needed once again: what *is* that virtue, about which you say the things that you say? Or is it your opinion that what I'm saying makes no sense?

MENO: In my opinion, at least, what you say is correct.

SOCRATES: Well, then, answer once again from the beginning. What do you assert virtue to be, both you and your comrade?

MENO: Socrates, before actually getting together with you, I used to

80a   hear nothing else than that you yourself are perplexed and make others perplexed as well. And now, in my opinion at any rate, you're bewitching and enchanting me with your potion and really casting a spell over me, so that I've become full of perplexity. In my opinion too you are in every way—if I may be permitted a little joke—in form[45] and other respects, most like that well-known stingray of the sea. For it too always makes anyone who may draw near it and touch it feel numb, and in my opinion you have now done some such thing to me.[46] For

80b   in truth I for my part feel a numbness in both my soul and my tongue, and I can't give you any answer. Yet countless times I've made a great many speeches about virtue before many—and very well too, in my opinion at least. But now I'm not able to say even what it is at all. And in my opinion your resolution not to sail away or to move from here is a good one,[47] for if as a stranger in another city you should do things of this sort, you would perhaps be carted off to jail as a sorcerer.

SOCRATES: You are a rascal, Meno, and almost tricked me.

MENO: How so in particular, Socrates?

80c   SOCRATES: I recognize for what reason you likened me to something.

MENO: Why is that, do you suppose?

SOCRATES: So that I might liken you to something in return! And this I know about all who are beautiful: that they delight in being likened to things; it's to their profit. For even the likenesses of the beautiful are beautiful, I think. But I won't liken you to anything in return.

45. Or, "look," "appearance": *eidos* (see n. 19).
46. All modern editors here bracket the verb *narkan* that appears in the mss. at this point, on the grounds that its usual intransitive meaning ("to be numb") is out of place.
47. See, e.g., *Crito* 52b, where Socrates is said to have left Athens only for compulsory military service.

As for me, if the stingray makes itself numb while it numbs others, I am like it. But if not, I'm not. For I don't make others perplexed while I myself am free of perplexity, but above all else I myself am perplexed and in this way I make others perplexed too. Even now I

80d   don't know what virtue is and yet you, perhaps, did know it before touching me but now are like one who doesn't know. Nonetheless I'm willing to examine with you and seek out together with you what in the world it is.

MENO: And in what way, Socrates, will you seek out that about which you don't know at all *what* it is? By setting out for yourself what sort of a thing, from among those that you don't know, will you make your inquiry? Or even if you happen right upon it, how will you know that this is that thing which you didn't know?

80e   SOCRATES: I understand the sort of thing you mean to say, Meno. Do you see how eristic is this argument you're spinning, that it isn't possible for a human being to seek out either what he knows or what he doesn't know? For that which he knows he wouldn't seek out—he knows it, and such a person has no need of a search—nor what he doesn't know, for he doesn't even know what he will seek out.

81a   MENO: So then is this argument nobly stated, in your opinion, Socrates?

SOCRATES: Not in mine, at least.

MENO: Can you say how so?

SOCRATES: For my part, I can. For I have heard both men and women wise in the divine matters—

MENO: Stating what account?[48]

SOCRATES: What's true, in my opinion, at least, and noble.

MENO: What is this account, and who are the ones saying it?

SOCRATES: The ones saying this are all those among both the priests and priestesses who've been concerned with being able to give an ac-

81b   count of the matters in their purview. But Pindar too says this, as do many other poets, so many as are divine. And these are the things they say; just examine whether in your opinion what they say is true. For they assert that the human soul is immortal and that at one time it comes to an end (what in fact is called[49] "dying"), that at another it comes into being once again but never perishes. So, they assert, on

48. Or "argument" (*logos*).
49. Literally, "they call"; the subject of the verb is unstated and is probably meant to be general, as at 81d.

account of these things one should live out one's life as piously as possible.

> For from whomsoever Persephone accepts atonement for the ancient grief,
>
> To the sun above, in the ninth year,
>
> 81c She returns their soul[50] again. From them arise glorious kings
>
> And men swift in strength and greatest in wisdom
>
> And for the rest of time, they are called among human beings holy[51] heroes.

Now, since the soul is immortal and has come to be many times and has seen both the things here and those in Hades[52]—in fact all things—there isn't anything it hasn't learned. As a result, its being able to recollect what pertains to virtue and other things is nothing to be wondered at, since it also knew them previously. For, nature as a 81d whole being akin and the soul having learned all things, nothing prevents someone, once he has recollected just one thing—what human beings call "learning"—to discover all else, if he is courageous and doesn't grow weary in the search. For searching and learning as a whole are recollection. One shouldn't be persuaded by that eristic account, for it would make us lazy, and it is pleasant to hear for those human beings who are soft. *This* account, by contrast, makes us ac-81e tive and ready to search. Trusting it to be true, I'm willing to inquire, together with you, into what virtue is.

MENO: Yes, Socrates. But how do you mean this, that we don't learn but that what we call learning is recollection? Can you teach me how this is so?

SOCRATES: I just now said, Meno, that you are a rascal, and now you're 82a asking if I can teach you—I who assert that there is no learning but only recollection—so that I might immediately come to sight as contradicting myself!

MENO: No, by Zeus, Socrates, I didn't speak with an eye to that but from customary habit![53] But if you can somehow indicate to me that it is as you say, do so.

SOCRATES: Well, it isn't easy, but nonetheless I'm willing to be eager

---

50. Reading, with the mss., *psychan* rather than the conjectural *psychas* ("souls").
51. Or, "pure," "unsullied." Commentators have generally assumed Pindar to be the author of these lines, but their authorship is uncertain.
52. Or, more precisely, in the house of Hades, the Greek underworld.
53. *Ethos*: see also 70b.

82b   for your sake. Just call over for me one of your many attendants there, whomever you like, so that I may demonstrate on him for you.

MENO: Certainly. [*To a nearby* SLAVE] Come here.

SOCRATES: Is he Greek, then, and does he speak Greek?

MENO: Absolutely. He was born in my household.

SOCRATES: So pay attention as to which of the two he appears to you to be doing—either recollecting or learning from me.

MENO: I'll do so.

SOCRATES: So tell me, slave, do you know that a square figure is like this? [SOCRATES *begins to draw a square.*]

SLAVE: I do indeed.

82c   SOCRATES: Is a square figure, then, one that has all these lines equal, being four in number [ABCD]?

SLAVE: Certainly.

SOCRATES: And aren't these lines that it has here through the middle [EF, GH] equal too?

SLAVE: Yes.

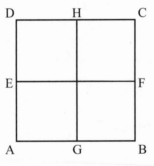

Figure 1

SOCRATES: Well, then, could such a figure be both larger and smaller?

SLAVE: Certainly.

SOCRATES: If, then, this side here [AB] were two feet and that one there [AD] two, how many square feet would the whole be? [*The* SLAVE *fails to answer.*] Examine it as follows. If it were two feet in this direction [AB], but only one foot in that direction [AE], isn't it the case that the figure would be one times two feet?

SLAVE: Yes.

82d   SOCRATES: But since it is two feet also in this direction [AD], surely it becomes two feet twice?

SLAVE: It does.

SOCRATES: Does it then become two times two feet?

SLAVE: Yes.

SOCRATES: Then how many is two times two feet? Calculate[54] and say.

SLAVE: Four, Socrates.

SOCRATES: Could there then come into being another figure twice the size of this one but like it in having all the lines equal, as this one does?

SLAVE: Yes.

SOCRATES: So how many square feet will it be?

SLAVE: Eight.

SOCRATES: Come, now, try to tell me how long each of the lines of that one will be. For this one here [AB] is two feet, but what would it be of that doubled figure?

SLAVE: It's clear, Socrates, that it would be double.

SOCRATES: Do you see, Meno, that I am teaching him nothing but am just asking him everything? And at this moment he supposes that he knows the sort of thing it is from which will arise an eight-square-foot figure. Or isn't that so in your opinion?

MENO: That's my opinion, at least.

SOCRATES: Does he know, then?

MENO: No indeed.

SOCRATES: But he supposes that it will arise from the doubled line?

MENO: Yes.

SOCRATES: Observe him making his recollections each in turn, as one ought to recollect. [SOCRATES *turns to speak to the* SLAVE.]

82e

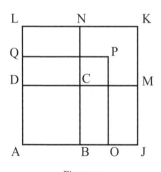

Figure 2

---

54. From the verb *logizomai*. The noun related to it (*logismos*) appears at 98a and 100b.

Now you tell me: do you assert that the doubled figure comes to
83a   be from the doubled line? [*The* SLAVE *fails to answer.*] I mean the following sort of thing: it shouldn't be large in this direction [AJ] and
short in that direction [AD], but let it be equal everywhere, as this one
is [ABCD]; just double the size of it, to eight square feet. But see if it
is still your opinion that it will arise from the doubled side.

SLAVE: It will, in my opinion at least.

SOCRATES: Does this line [AJ], then, become double this one [AB], if
we add to it another as big as it, here [BJ]?

SLAVE: Certainly.

SOCRATES: So from this, you assert, will arise the eight-square-foot figure, if there come to be four sides of this size?

SLAVE: Yes.

83b   SOCRATES: Let's inscribe, then, four equal sides from it [AJKL]. Surely
you assert that this here would be eight square feet?

SLAVE: Certainly.

SOCRATES: There are then these four in it, each of which [BJMC,
CMKN, DCNL] is equal to this four-square-foot figure [ABCD]?

SLAVE: Yes.

SOCRATES: So how big does it become? Wouldn't it be four times this
much?

SLAVE: Of course.

SOCRATES: Then is that which is four times this much double?

SLAVE: No, by Zeus.

SOCRATES: But how many?

SLAVE: Four times as much.

83c   SOCRATES: So from the doubled line, slave, a figure not twice but four
times the size comes to be.

SLAVE: What you say is true.

SOCRATES: For four times four is sixteen, no?

SLAVE: Yes.

SOCRATES: And from what sort of line would an eight-square-foot figure come to be? Didn't the one four times as big [AJKL] come from
this line [AJ]?

SLAVE: I say that's so.

SOCRATES: And doesn't this quarter[55] here [ABCD] come from this
half [AB]?

---

55. Reading *tetarton* with the mss. and some editors instead of the conjectural *tetrapoun*
("And doesn't this four-square-foot one . . . ?").

SLAVE: Yes.

SOCRATES: Well, then. Isn't the eight-square-foot figure double this one here [ABCD], but half of this [AJKL]? [*The* SLAVE *fails to answer.*][56] Won't it arise from one greater than this line [AB] but less than that one [AJ], or not?

83d   SLAVE: That's so, in my opinion at least.

SOCRATES: Fine[57]—keep answering according to your opinion. And tell me: wasn't this side here [AB] two feet, that one [AJ] four?

SLAVE: Yes.

SOCRATES: Then the side of the eight-square-foot figure ought to be greater than this two-foot line here [AB] but less than the four-foot line [AJ].

SLAVE: It ought to be.

83e   SOCRATES: So try to say how big you assert it to be.

SLAVE: Three feet.

SOCRATES: Then if in fact it is three feet, will we add half of this [AB] again, and will it be three feet [AO]? For this here is two [AB]; that one [BO], one. And from here, similarly, this is two feet here [AD]; that one [DQ], one. And this is the figure that you assert comes to be [AOPQ].

SLAVE: Yes.

SOCRATES: Then if it is three here [AO] and three there [AQ], the whole figure comes to be three times three feet?

SLAVE: It appears so.

SOCRATES: And three times three are how many square feet?

SLAVE: Nine.

SOCRATES: But the double ought to have been how many square feet?

SLAVE: Eight.

SOCRATES: So the eight-square-foot figure doesn't yet come to be from the three-foot line, either.

SLAVE: No, it doesn't.

SOCRATES: But from what sort of line? Try to tell us precisely. And if
84a   you don't want to count out the line, just point out from what sort.

SLAVE: But by Zeus, Socrates, for my part I don't know!

SOCRATES: Are you considering again, Meno, to what point he has already proceeded in his recollecting? To begin with he didn't know what the line of the eight-square-foot figure is—just as he still doesn't

---

56. No reply is recorded in the principal mss. or in the Latin of Aristippus, but an affirmative reply has been added in one ms.

57. *Kalōs* (see n. 14).

know—but he then *supposed* that he did know it and confidently answered as though he did and didn't believe that he was perplexed. But now he does believe that he is perplexed, and just as he doesn't 84b know in fact, so he doesn't even suppose that he knows.

MENO: What you say is true.

SOCRATES: So is he now in a better condition concerning the matter he didn't know?

MENO: This too is so in my opinion.

SOCRATES: In making him perplexed and feel numb, as the stingray does, surely we didn't harm him at all?

MENO: Not in my opinion, at least.

SOCRATES: Indeed, we've done him some benefit, as is likely, with a view to discovering how the matter stands. For now he might even gladly inquire because he doesn't know, but then he easily supposed that he would speak well, before many and many times, about the 84c doubled figure, to the effect that the line ought to be doubled in length.

MENO: It's likely.

SOCRATES: So do you think that he would have attempted to inquire into or learn that which he supposed he knew but didn't, before he fell into perplexity by having come to believe that he didn't know, and before he felt a longing to know?

MENO: Not in my opinion, Socrates.

SOCRATES: He was benefited, then, by feeling numb?

MENO: In my opinion.

SOCRATES: Examine, then, what he will in fact discover, starting from this perplexity, by inquiring with me—though I'm doing nothing other than asking him questions and am not teaching him. And be on 84d guard if somewhere you discover me teaching him and explaining things for him, rather than just asking him about his opinions. [SOCRATES *returns to the* SLAVE.]

Now you tell me. Isn't this our four-square-foot figure [ABCD]? Do you understand?

SLAVE: I do indeed.

SOCRATES: Might we set down in addition to it another one here equal to it [BJMC]?

SLAVE: Yes.

SOCRATES: And a third one here [CMKN], equal to each of these?

SLAVE: Yes.

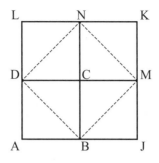

Figure 3

SOCRATES: Might we add to this one in the corner, then, to fill it up [DCNL]?

SLAVE: Certainly.

SOCRATES: Surely, then, there would arise these four equal figures?

84e SLAVE: Yes.

SOCRATES: What then? How many times greater does this whole here [AJKL] become than this one [ABCD]?

SLAVE: Four times.

SOCRATES: But we had to bring the double into being. Or don't you remember?

SLAVE: Certainly.

SOCRATES: Now does this line that goes from corner to corner [BD] cut

85a each of these figures in two?

SLAVE: Yes.

SOCRATES: Then do these four equal lines come to be [BD, BM, MN, DN], enclosing this figure here [BMND]?

SLAVE: They do.

SOCRATES: So examine it: how big is this figure?

SLAVE: I don't understand.

SOCRATES: Hasn't each line cut off the inner half of each of these four [ABCD, BJMC, CMKN, DCNL]? Or not?

SLAVE: Yes.

SOCRATES: So how many, then, of this size [BCD] are present in this [BMND]?

SLAVE: Four.

SOCRATES: And how many in this one here [ABCD]?

SLAVE: Two.

SOCRATES: And what is four in relation to two?

SLAVE: Double.

SOCRATES: This [BMND], then, becomes how many feet?

85b SLAVE: Eight square feet.

SOCRATES: From what sort of line?

SLAVE: From this one [BD].

SOCRATES: From the one that cuts from corner to corner of the four-square-foot figure?

SLAVE: Yes.

SOCRATES: And the sophists call this "diameter." So if the name of this is diameter, it would be from the diameter, as you assert, Meno's slave, that the doubled figure would come to be.

SLAVE: Certainly, Socrates.

SOCRATES: What is your opinion, Meno? Is there any opinion he gave in response that was not his own?

85c MENO: No, they were his own.

SOCRATES: And yet he didn't *know*, as we asserted a little before.

MENO: What you say is true.

SOCRATES: But the opinions themselves were present in him. Or not?

MENO: Yes.

SOCRATES: In one who doesn't know, then, about whatever it may be that he doesn't know, there are present true opinions about those things that he doesn't know?[58]

MENO: It appears so.

SOCRATES: And now, at any rate, these very opinions have just been stirred up in him, like a dream. And if someone will ask him these same things many times and in many ways, you know that he will 85d end up having knowledge[59] about them no less precisely than anyone.

MENO: That's likely.

SOCRATES: So then without anyone having taught him but just having asked him questions, he will possess knowledge, he himself recovering the knowledge from within himself?

MENO: Yes.

---

58. The reading of the mss. Schleiermacher among others deletes the final phrase, "about those things he doesn't know?" Bluck ad loc. and Klein, *Commentary,* 176, accept the reading of the mss.

59. Or, "science," "knowledge in the strict sense" (*epistēmē*).

SOCRATES: Isn't his recovering knowledge within himself recollecting?

MENO: Certainly.

SOCRATES: Then with respect to the knowledge that he now has, didn't he either get hold of it at some point or have it always?

MENO: Yes.

SOCRATES: Then if he had it always, he was always also a knower. But if he got hold of it at a certain point, he would not have done so in
85e   this life, at least. Or has someone taught him geometry? For with respect to geometry as a whole, and all the other subjects of learning, he will do these same things. Is there anyone, then, who has taught him all things? It's just[60] for you to know, I suppose, especially since he was born and raised in your household.

MENO: But for my part I do know that no one ever taught him.

SOCRATES: But he has these opinions, or doesn't he?

MENO: Necessarily, Socrates, as it appears.

SOCRATES: But if he didn't get hold of them in this life, isn't it clear by
86a   now that he got them and learned them in some other time?

MENO: That appears so.

SOCRATES: So this is the time when he wasn't a human being?

MENO: Yes.

SOCRATES: If, then, in both whatever time he is and whatever time he is not a human being, true opinions will be present in him that come to be knowledge[61] once they've been roused by questioning—then will his soul always be in a state of having learned? For it's clear that, for all time, he either is or is not a human being.

MENO: That appears so.

86b   SOCRATES: So if the truth about the beings is always present for us in the soul, would the soul be immortal such that, with respect to what you now happen not to know—and this is what you don't remember—you should be confident in attempting to inquire into it and recollect it?

MENO: In my opinion what you say is well spoken, Socrates—I don't know quite how.

SOCRATES: In mine too, Meno. As for the other points, at least, I wouldn't insist very much on behalf of the argument; but that by sup-

60. Or, perhaps, "It's your obligation" (*dikaios*).
61. Plural in the Greek.

posing one ought to inquire into things he doesn't know, we would be better and more manly and less lazy than if we should suppose either that it's impossible to discover those things that we don't know

86c   or that we ought not inquire into them—about *this* I certainly would do battle, if I could, both in speech and in deed.

MENO: This too is well said, in my opinion, Socrates.

SOCRATES: Do you want, then, since we are of one mind that it is necessary to inquire into what one doesn't know—are we to attempt to inquire in common into what in the world virtue is?

MENO: Certainly. And yet, Socrates, for my part I'd most gladly examine and hear about that which I first raised as a question, namely whether one ought to take it to be something teachable, or whether

86d   virtue comes to be present in human beings by nature, or in whatever other way it does so.

SOCRATES: Well, if I ruled not only myself but you as well, Meno, we wouldn't examine whether virtue is something teachable or isn't something teachable before we inquired in the first place into what it itself is. And since you don't even attempt to rule yourself—so that you can be free, I suppose—but attempt to rule me and do rule me in fact, I'll yield to you. For what ought I to do?

It seems necessary, then, to examine what *sort* of a thing something

86e   is when we don't yet know *what* it is. If nothing else, at least relax your rule over me a little and agree to examine whether it is something teachable or however it may be, on the basis of a hypothesis. I mean by "on the basis of a hypothesis," this: just as the geometers often examine, when someone asks them about a given area[62]—for example, whether it is possible for this area to be inscribed as a triangle within that circle— someone might say: "I don't yet know whether

87a   this is such [as to be inscribed in this way], but I think I have a kind of hypothesis that is advantageous with a view to the matter at hand, about as follows:[63] if this area is such that, when it is applied to the

---

62. Or "figure," here and throughout (*chorion*).

63. These difficult remarks have occasioned much commentary, and Bluck's caution should probably be heeded: "It has been very reasonably claimed . . . that the identity of the theorem is strictly speaking unimportant" (Bluck 441). For a helpful overview, see Bluck's appendix (441–61) and R. W. Sharples, *Plato's Meno* (Chicago: Bolchazy-Carducci, 1985), 158–60. According to W. R. M. Lamb (*Laches Protagoras Meno Euthydemus*, vol. 4, Loeb Classical Library [Cambridge: Harvard University Press, 1923], 325), the problem is one of inscribing in a circle a triangle (BDG) equal in area to a given rectangle (ABCD). See Figure 4.

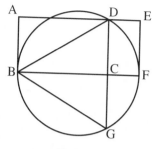

Figure 4

given line[64] [of the circle], it falls short[65] by an area similar to the very one being applied to it, it is my opinion that one thing results and another, in turn, if it is unable to undergo these things. So, by using a hypothesis, I'm willing to tell you the result of inscribing it within a circle, whether it is impossible or not."

87b

Let's make a hypothesis in this way about virtue as well, since we don't know either what it is or what sort of a thing it is, and let's examine whether it is something teachable or is not something teachable, by speaking as follows: what sort of thing, among the beings pertaining to the soul, would virtue have to be for it to be either something teachable or something not teachable? First, if it is different from the kind of thing knowledge is, is it something teachable or not—or as we were just now saying, something recollectible? Let it make no difference to us which of the two names we use: is it something teachable? Or is this at least clear to everyone: a human being is taught nothing other than knowledge?

87c

MENO: That's my opinion, at any rate.

SOCRATES: But if virtue is a kind of knowledge, it's clear that it would be something teachable.

MENO: Of course.

SOCRATES: We disposed of this quickly, then—that being of the one sort it is something teachable; of the other sort, not.

MENO: Certainly.

SOCRATES: So we ought to examine this next, as is likely: whether virtue is knowledge or other than knowledge.

64. That is, the diameter (BF).
65. That is, it falls short of the rectangle on the diameter (ABFE).

87d   MENO: In my opinion, at least, this is the next thing that has to be examined.

SOCRATES: And what then? Do we assert that it itself, virtue, is anything other than good, and does this remain[66] our hypothesis, that it itself is good?

MENO: Certainly.

SOCRATES: If, then, there is something that is good and other than and separate from knowledge, perhaps virtue would not be a kind of knowledge. But if there is nothing good which knowledge does not encompass, in suspecting that it is a kind of knowledge we would suspect correctly.

MENO: That is so.

SOCRATES: And surely it is by means of virtue that we are good?

87e   MENO: Yes.

SOCRATES: And if we're good, we're advantageous[67]—for all the good things are advantageous, no?

MENO: Yes.

SOCRATES: And virtue is indeed something advantageous?

MENO: That's necessary on the basis of the things agreed to.

SOCRATES: So let's take up each point in turn and examine what the sorts of things are that are to our advantage. Health, we assert, and strength and beauty and of course wealth: we say that these things, and those like them, are advantageous, no?

MENO: Yes.

88a   SOCRATES: But we assert that these same things sometimes also do harm—or do you speak in a manner different from this?

MENO: No, but in this way.

SOCRATES: So examine this: when what guides each of these are they to our advantage, and when what guides do they do harm? Isn't it when correct usage guides, they are to our advantage, and when not, they do harm?

MENO: Certainly.

SOCRATES: Let's examine in addition, then, the things pertaining to the soul as well. Do you call something "moderation" and "justice" and "courage" and "docility" and "memory" and "magnificence," and all things of this sort?

66. From the verb *menō* ("to stay in one's place," hence to be steady, stable), itself reminiscent of Meno's name (*Menōn*).
67. Or, "useful," "beneficial" (*ōphelima*).

88b   MENO: I do indeed.

SOCRATES: So examine whether, in your opinion, some of these that are not knowledge but are other than knowledge at one time do harm but at another are advantageous. For example, courage—if courage is not prudence[68] but a certain sort of boldness.[69] Isn't it the case that when a human being is bold without intellect,[70] it is to his harm, but when with intellect, it is to his advantage?

MENO: Yes.

88c   SOCRATES: This holds similarly, then, also for moderation and docility: are things learned and things acquired by training advantageous when accompanied by intellect but harmful when not accompanied by intellect?

MENO: Yes, absolutely.

SOCRATES: In sum, then, do all the undertakings and acts of endurance of the soul issue in happiness when prudence guides, but when imprudence[71] guides, in the contrary?

MENO: That's likely.

SOCRATES: If, then, virtue is one of the things in the soul and it is necessarily advantageous, it must be prudence, since in fact all the things pertaining to the soul are, themselves by themselves, neither advantageous nor harmful, but when prudence or imprudence is present in addition, they become either harmful or advantageous.[72] So according to this account, virtue, because it is advantageous, must be a certain prudence.

MENO: That's my opinion, at any rate.

SOCRATES: And in addition, the other things too we were just now speaking of as being sometimes good and sometimes harmful—wealth and things of that sort—isn't it the case that, just as when prudence guides the rest of the soul it makes the things of the soul advantageous, as we saw,[73] but when imprudence guides it makes

88d

---

68. Or, "understanding," "judgment," especially in regard to practical matters (*phronēsis*).

69. Or, "confidence" (*tharros*); see also *Protagoras* 349e and context.

70. Or, "mind" (*nous*), here and throughout.

71. Or, "foolishness" (*aphrosunē*).

72. Literally, "they become harmful and advantageous."

73. This phrase does not appear in the Greek but attempts to convey the sense of the two "philosophic imperfects" that do appear here and that serve to summarize previous arguments. A more literal rendering would be: "just as when prudence guides the rest of the soul it was making the things of the soul advantageous, but when imprudence guides it was making them harmful."

88e   them harmful, so also when the soul in turn correctly uses these things and guides them it makes them advantageous, but when incorrectly, harmful?

MENO: Certainly.

SOCRATES: And the soul with good sense guides correctly, the foolish one mistakenly?

MENO: That is so.

SOCRATES: It is possible, then, to speak in this way in all cases: for a human being all other things depend on the soul, but the things of the soul itself depend on prudence, if they are to be good. And by this

89a   account the advantageous would be prudence. And do we assert that virtue is something advantageous?

MENO: Certainly.

SOCRATES: Do we assert, then, that virtue is prudence, either in whole or in part?[74]

MENO: In my opinion, Socrates, what's being said is nobly spoken.

SOCRATES: Then if these things are so, those who are good would not be by nature.[75]

MENO: Not in my opinion.

89b   SOCRATES: For if that were so, I suppose, the following too would be the case: if those who are good did come to be by nature, there would, I suppose, be men who recognized for us those among the young whose natures are good. These we would take aside, once they had pointed them out, and guard them in the Acropolis,[76] having them sealed up much more than we do gold so that no one might corrupt[77] them but rather, once they come of age, they might become useful to the cities.[78]

MENO: Well, that's likely, at least, Socrates.

SOCRATES: Since, then, the good don't become good by nature, do

89c   they become such by learning?

---

74. The phrase "either in whole or in part" may qualify "virtue" or "prudence." Bluck (ad loc.) suggests the latter.

75. One ms. reads: "those who are good would not be good by nature."

76. Public monies were kept in the temples on the Athenian Acropolis.

77. The same verb (*diaphtheirō*) is used in the indictment against Socrates: see Diogenes Laertius 2.40.

78. The grammar of the first part of this two-part purpose clause is ambiguous; it may be translated either as an imperfect, as in the text, or as an aorist ("so that no one might have corrupted them"); the implication of the sentence as a whole is that, since such good natures do exist and are not in fact sealed away, "they are not protected from corruption" (Sharples ad loc.).

MENO: In my opinion, that's necessary now. And it's clear, Socrates, according to the hypothesis, that if in fact virtue is knowledge, it is something teachable.

SOCRATES: Perhaps so, by Zeus. But maybe we didn't agree to this nobly?

MENO: And yet it was our opinion just a moment ago, at least, that it was nobly stated.

SOCRATES: But it ought to be our opinion that it was nobly stated not only just a moment ago, but now and in the future too, if there is to be something sound about it.

89d MENO: Well, what then? With a view to what are you dissatisfied with it and distrust virtue's being knowledge?

SOCRATES: I'll tell you, Meno. As for its being something teachable, if in fact it is knowledge, this I don't retract as being ignobly stated. But examine whether in your opinion it is fitting that I distrust its being knowledge.

Tell me this: if any matter whatever is teachable, not only virtue, isn't it necessary for there to be both teachers and students of it?

MENO: In my opinion, at least.

89e SOCRATES: Then does the contrary hold in turn: if there should be something that has neither teachers nor students of it, would we conjecture nobly in conjecturing that it isn't something teachable?

MENO: That is so. But isn't it your opinion that there are teachers of virtue?

SOCRATES: Well, although I've inquired many times whether there are any teachers of it, and although I make every effort, I'm unable to discover any. Yet I inquire together with many, and especially with those who, as I suppose, are most experienced in the matter. And even now, Meno, Anytus[79] here has sat down beside us at an opportune[80] time;

90a let's give him a share in the inquiry. And it's fitting that we should do so: to begin with, Anytus here has as a father the wealthy and wise Anthemion,[81] who became wealthy not automatically or because someone gave it to him—like that one who just recently got hold of

---

79. A leading democratic politician in Athens who was to become one of the three official accusers of Socrates. See *Apology of Socrates* 18b3, 23e3–24a, as well as Xenophon, *Apology of Socrates to the Jury* 29–31.

80. Literally, "noble" or "fine" (*kalos*).

81. Little is known of him apart from what Socrates here tells us. According to the scholiast on *Apology of Socrates* 18b, he made his fortune through the manufacture of leather, a most ignoble profession.

the money of Polycrates,[82] Ismenias the Theban[83]—but acquired it through his own wisdom and diligence. In addition, opinion has it that he isn't in other respects an arrogant citizen or a puffed up and difficult one but is an orderly and well-behaved man. Further, he

90b   reared this fellow well and educated him, as the opinion of the Athenian multitude has it: they elect him, at any rate, to the greatest offices. So it is just to investigate with those of this sort whether or not teachers of virtue exist and who they are.

You, then, Anytus, inquire together with us, with me and your own guest-friend[84] Meno here, who the teachers of this matter are. Examine it as follows: if we should want Meno here to become a good

90c   physician, to whom would we send him as teachers? Wouldn't it be to the physicians?

ANYTUS: Certainly.

SOCRATES: And what if we should want him to become a good shoemaker?[85] Wouldn't it be to the shoemakers?

ANYTUS: Yes.

SOCRATES: And so on with the rest?

ANYTUS: Certainly.

SOCRATES: So tell me the following about the same things once again: we assert that, in sending this one here to physicians, we would do so nobly, provided we want him to become a physician. When we say

90d   this, do we mean that we would be sensible[86] in sending him to those who both lay claim to the art (rather than to those who do not) and take pay for this very thing, presenting themselves as teachers to anyone who wants to go to them and learn? Wouldn't we, by looking to these things, send him off nobly?

---

82. Polycrates was the name of a tyrant from Samos, of the sixth century B.C.; see Herodotus 3.39 and following. The expression may have become proverbial for great wealth, but Bluck suggests that the Polycrates in question was an Athenian writer of democratic sympathies who bribed Ismenias to support the democracy in Athens.

83. The meaning of this reference is uncertain. Some have suggested that the Ismenias mentioned was the leader of the democratic party at Thebes who received a bribe for stirring up war against Sparta in Greece (see Bluck ad loc.; Xenophon, *Hellenica* 3.5.1). But this episode occurred in 395 B.C., and the dramatic date of the dialogue would seem to be 402 B.C. J. S. Morrison ("Meno of Pharsalus, Polycrates, and Ismenias," *Classical Quarterly* 36 [1942]: 57 and following), followed by Bluck, suggests an earlier act of bribery (see the preceding note) compatible with the dramatic date of 402 B.C..

84. *Xenos*: see n. 41.

85. Literally, "leather cutter." Socrates may thus be alluding to the (ignoble) occupation of Anytus' family (see n. 81 and Xenophon, *Apology of Socrates to the Jury* 29).

86. A verb linked with the word for "moderation" (*sōphrosunē*).

ANYTUS: Yes.

SOCRATES: Do these same things hold, then, concerning aulos-play-
90e   ing[87] and the rest? It is very unintelligent for those who want to make
someone an aulos player to be unwilling to send him to those who
claim to teach the art and take pay for doing so but instead to trouble certain others[88] who neither pretend to be teachers nor have even
one student of that subject which we think the one we send should
learn from them. Isn't that very irrational, in your opinion?

ANYTUS: Yes, by Zeus, that is my opinion, and it's ignorant besides.

SOCRATES: Nobly said. Well, then, it's now possible[89] for you to de-
91a   liberate in common with me concerning this guest-friend here, Meno.
For, Anytus, he has for a long time been saying to me that he desires
that wisdom and virtue by means of which human beings nobly manage both households and cities and tend to their own parents and
know how both to receive and to send off citizens and guest-friends
in a manner worthy of a good man. With a view to this virtue, then,
91b   examine to whom we might send him and do so correctly. Or is it indeed clear, according to the recent argument, that it is to those who
claim to be teachers of virtue and who present themselves as being
available to anyone among the Greeks who wants to learn, having established and charging a fee for this?

ANYTUS: And who do you say these are, Socrates?

SOCRATES: Doubtless you too[90] know that they are those whom people call "sophists."

91c   ANYTUS: Heracles! Hush, Socrates![91] May no madness of this kind
seize anyone among my family[92] or relatives or friends, be he a local
or foreigner, so that he goes to them to be ruined! For *they* are plainly
the ruin and corruption of those who associate with them!

SOCRATES: How do you mean, Anytus? Do they alone, among those
laying a claim to know how to perform some benefaction, differ so

87. The aulos was a reed instrument not unlike the modern oboe.
88. I follow Bluck, Schanz (*Platonis opera quae feruntur omnia* [Lipsiae, 1881]), Thompson,
and Sharples in deleting at this point a difficult phrase that appears in the mss. and that
could be translated, "in his search to learn from those."
89. Or, "permissible."
90. Or, perhaps, "even you."
91. Literally, "speak good omens" (*euphēmeō*). The verb is used when another has said
something highly inappropriate or even blasphemous.
92. Reading *suggenōn* with Croiset, Verdenius, and the mss. rather than Burnet's conjectural
g'emōn ("any of my own, whether relatives or friends").

much from the rest that they not only don't do any benefit, as do the others, to whatever one may entrust to them, but to the contrary even
91d   corrupt it? And they deem it right to charge money openly for this?

Now, I can't see my way to believing you, for I know one man, Protagoras,[93] who acquired more money from this wisdom than both Pheidias[94]—who produced such notably beautiful works—and ten other sculptors taken together. And indeed, what you say is amazing:[95] those who work on old shoes and mend cloaks wouldn't be able to escape notice for thirty days if they were to give the cloaks and
91e   shoes back in a worse condition than when they received them but would soon perish by stoning, if they were to do things of that sort; whereas Protagoras, who corrupted those who associated with him and sent them back in a worse condition than when he received them for more than forty years, escaped the notice of the whole of Greece— for I think he died at the age of nearly seventy, being forty years in the practice of the art—and in *all* this time, still to this very day, he hasn't ceased being well thought of! And not only Protagoras but
92a   very many others besides, both those who came before him and those who are still alive even now.

So are we to assert, then, according to your account, that they themselves know they trick and ruin the young, or that have they escaped even their own notice in doing so? And will we deem them to be so mad—those who, some assert, are the wisest of human beings?

ANYTUS: They are *far* from being mad, Socrates. Much more so are those of the young who give them money—and still more than they,
92b   those who allow them to do so,[96] the relatives. But above all, the cities that permit them to enter and don't banish them, whether it's some foreigner who attempts to do some such thing or a local!

SOCRATES: Has one of the sophists done you some injustice, Anytus? Or why are you so harsh toward them?

ANYTUS: By Zeus! *I* have never associated with any one of them, and neither would I allow any of my own to do so!

---

93. As Socrates goes on to indicate, Protagoras was one of the most famous of the sophists or teachers of his day. Plato records a visit of his to Athens in the *Protagoras* and has Socrates repeat an important aspect of Protagoras' teaching in the *Theaetetus*.

94. Pheidias of Athens was the most celebrated sculptor of his day whose works adorned the Parthenon.

95. The word Socrates uses here (*teras*) can mean a sign or wonder from heaven and even "monster."

96. The phrase may also mean: "those who entrust [the young to the sophists]."

SOCRATES: Are you then completely without experience of the men?

ANYTUS: And may I remain so!

92c   SOCRATES: How then, you daimonic[97] fellow, could you know whether there is something good or useless[98] in this matter when you are completely without experience of it?

ANYTUS: Easily! I know, at any rate, who they are—whether or not I'm without experience of them!

SOCRATES: Perhaps you are a prophet, Anytus. For I should wonder how else you know about them, on the basis of what you yourself say.

But in any case we aren't inquiring into who those are to whom
92d   Meno might go and become depraved—let these be, if you like, the sophists. Rather, say to us—and do this paternal comrade here a good turn by telling it—who those are to whom he might go in so great a city and become worthy of account with respect to the virtue that I just now went through.

ANYTUS: Why don't *you* tell him!

SOCRATES: But I did speak of those whom I supposed to be teachers of these things, but I happen to make no sense, as you assert. And per-
92e   haps you are making sense. So you in your turn state for him to which of the Athenians he is to go. Say the name of anyone you like.

ANYTUS: But why must he hear the name of a single human being? For there isn't anyone among the noble and good[99] Athenians he might come across who won't make him better than the sophists would, if in fact he's willing to obey them.

SOCRATES: Did these noble and good ones become such spontaneously,[100] and although they learned from no one they are nonethe-
93a   less able to teach others these things that they themselves didn't learn?

ANYTUS: For my part, I fully expect that they too learned from their predecessors, who were noble and good. Or isn't it your opinion that many good men have arisen in this city?[101]

---

97. A daimon was, at least in Plato and afterward, a being between gods and human beings. Socrates claimed to have a "daimonic" voice that checked him when he was about to do something ill-advised (see, e.g., *Republic* 496c; *Apology of Socrates* 27c–e; *Theages* 128d and following).

98. *Phlauros*: bad, often the contrary of *chrēstos* ("good," "useful," "worthy").

99. The usual translation of the Greek *kaloi kagathoi* is "gentlemen," but its more literal meaning ought to be kept in mind.

100. Or, "automatically" (*automatou*), as it is translated in its only other appearance in the dialogue (90a).

101. The word order of the Greek puts some stress on "men" (*andres*).

SOCRATES: It is my opinion at least, Anytus, both that there are those good at the political things here and that they were such in the past no less than they are at present. But they haven't also been good teachers of their own virtue, have they? For it is this that our argument is about—not if there are or are not good men here, nor if there were any in the past, but rather we've been examining for a long time whether virtue is something teachable. And in examining this we are examining the following: did the good men, both those at present and those in the past, know how to bestow on another as well that virtue with respect to which they themselves were good, or can this not be bestowed on a human being nor be taken from one and given to another? This is what we've been inquiring into for a long time, Meno and I.

93b

So examine it as follows, on the basis of your own account: wouldn't you assert that Themistocles[102] was a good man?

93c

ANYTUS: I certainly would, he above all.

SOCRATES: And [would you assert as well], then, that if anybody was a good teacher of his own virtue, he was?

ANYTUS: For my part, I think so—if, that is, he wanted to.

SOCRATES: But do you think that he wouldn't have wanted certain others to become noble and good, and especially, I suppose, his own son? Or do you think that he bore ill will against him and intentionally did not bestow on him that virtue with respect to which he himself was good? Or haven't you heard that Themistocles had his son Cleophantus taught to be a good horseman? At any rate, he used to be able to remain standing upright on horseback and to throw a javelin while standing on horseback, and do many other amazing deeds, which Themistocles had him taught to do and with respect to which he made him wise—so many things as depended on having good teachers. Or haven't you heard these things from the elders?

93d

ANYTUS: I have heard them.

SOCRATES: No one would have alleged, then, that his son's nature, at any rate, was bad.

93e

ANYTUS: Perhaps not.

SOCRATES: What then about this: have you ever heard from anyone,

102. A leading democratic statesman in Athens (c. 528–462 B.C.), largely responsible for the naval strategy that led to the Greeks' triumph over the Persian forces of Xerxes. His political rivals later gained ascendancy in Athens, however, and he was eventually exiled and sentenced to death in absentia. See Thucydides 1.74, 93, 135–38 and Plutarch, *Themistocles*.

young or old, that Cleophantus, son of Themistocles, became a good and wise man in the respects in which his father was?

ANYTUS: No indeed.

SOCRATES: Do we suppose, then, that he wanted to educate his son in those things, but that he didn't want to make him any better than his neighbors in that wisdom with respect to which he himself was wise—if in fact virtue were something teachable?

ANYTUS: Perhaps not, by Zeus!

SOCRATES: Such, then, was your teacher of virtue, whom you too[103] agree was among the best of the forbears. But let's examine another,

94a   Aristides[104] son of Lysimachus. Or don't you agree that he was good?

ANYTUS: I do indeed, doubtless in every respect.

SOCRATES: Well, he too had his own son, Lysimachus, educated in all the things that depend on teachers, in the noblest manner of any Athenian. But in your opinion did he make him a better man than anyone else whatever? For I guess you've associated with him, and you see what he is like. [ANYTUS *fails to respond.*]

94b   But if you want, take Pericles, so magnificently wise a man. Do you know that he reared two sons, Paralus and Xanthippus?[105]

ANYTUS: I do indeed.

SOCRATES: Well, these, as you too[106] know, he had educated to be horsemen inferior to none of the Athenians, and had them instructed in music and exercise and all that depends on art such that they were inferior to none. Didn't he want to make them good men, then? In my opinion he did want to, but it may not be something teachable.

But so that you not think this matter was impossible for just a few of the Athenians, and the paltriest ones at that, consider that Thucy-

94c   dides[107] in turn reared two sons, Melesias and Stephanus. These he had educated well in other respects too, but he had them taught in particular how to wrestle in the noblest manner of any of the Athenians—for he gave the one to Xanthias, the other to Eudorus, men

---

103. Or, perhaps, "whom even you." The word translated "too" in the text (*kai*) is omitted in one ms.

104. An illustrious Athenian statesman and general who fought bravely against the Persians. Unlike the rather wily Themistocles, his contemporary, Aristides was famous for his honesty.

105. Both appear in the *Protagoras* (315a).

106. Or, "as even you know."

107. Not the historian of the Peloponnesian War but the leader of the aristocratic party in Athens opposed to Pericles' democratic party. His son Melesias appears in Plato's *Laches*.

who were, I suppose, held to be the noblest wrestlers of the time. Or don't you remember?

ANYTUS: I do indeed—I've heard about it.

SOCRATES: So is it clear that, since he had his sons taught those things he had to spend money for, he never would have failed to teach them those things he need not have incurred any expense for in order to make them good men—if that were something teachable? But perhaps Thucydides was a paltry fellow and didn't have the greatest number of friends among Athenians and the allies? In fact he was of a great house and had great power both in the city and among the rest of the Greeks such that, if in fact this were something teachable, he would have discovered who was going to make his sons good—someone either native or foreign—if he himself were not at leisure to do so on account of the attention he paid to the city. But, Anytus, my comrade, virtue may not be something teachable.

ANYTUS: Socrates, in my opinion you speak ill of people lightly. So I would advise you, if you're willing to be persuaded by me, to be careful: perhaps it is easy in another city too to harm people or to benefit them, but in *this* one it is very easy indeed.[108] But I think you yourself know this as well.

SOCRATES: Meno, in my opinion Anytus is angry, and I don't in the least wonder why. For, in the first place, he supposes that I am slandering these men; and, second, he believes that he himself is also one of them. But if he ever understands what sort of a thing "speaking ill"[109] is, he'll cease to be angry. As things stand, he is ignorant of it.

But you tell me: aren't there noble and good men in your parts too?

MENO: Certainly.

SOCRATES: What, then? Are these willing to make themselves available to the young as teachers? And to agree both that they are teachers and that virtue is something teachable?

MENO: No, by Zeus, Socrates, but at one time you might hear from them that it is something teachable, at another that it's not.

---

108. The reading of the mss. Burnet and Croiset read the comparative *raon*, as suggested by Buttman (*Platonis dialogi IV Meno Crito Alcibiades uterque* [Berlin, 1830]): "it is perhaps easier in another city too to harm people rather than to benefit them, but in *this* one it is very easy indeed." For a defense of the mss., see Bluck ad loc., which is accepted by Klein, *Commentary*, 233 n. 42.

109. Literally, "speaking badly" (as also at 94e): Socrates plays on the literal meaning of the phrase.

SOCRATES: Are we to assert, then, that these are teachers of this matter, they who don't agree even about this very thing?

MENO: Not in my opinion, Socrates.

SOCRATES: So what then? Are those sophists, who alone profess to be
such, teachers of virtue in your opinion?

95c   MENO: In fact I especially admire Gorgias for this, Socrates: you
would never hear him claiming this. Rather, he even ridicules the others, when he hears them claiming to do so. He thinks instead that it's
at speaking that one ought to make people clever.

SOCRATES: So not even the sophists are teachers in your opinion?

MENO: I can't say, Socrates. For I myself have experienced what in fact
the many have: at one time it is my opinion that they are, at another
that they aren't.

SOCRATES: And do you know that not only you and the other political men are at one time of the opinion that it is something teachable

95d   and at another that it is not, but that the poet Theognis[110] too says
these same things? Do you know that?

MENO: In which verses?

SOCRATES: In the elegiacs, where he says:

> With them drink and eat, and with them
> Be seated, and be pleasing to them whose power is great.
> For from the noble (*esthlōn*)[111] you will be taught noble (*esthla*) things;
> but if with the bad

95e
> You mingle, you will lose even the intellect you have.[112]

Do you know that in *these* lines he is speaking as though virtue is
something teachable?

MENO: It appears so, at least.

SOCRATES: But in others, by contrast, a little further on, he asserts:

> But if understanding could be produced and instilled in a man

He says roughly that those who are capable of doing this,

> Would earn much great pay

And,

> Never from a good father would there have arisen a bad man,

---

110. Elegiac poet (fl. 544–41 B.C.) from Megara.

111. Not the word elsewhere translated as "noble" (*kalos*) but the more poetic *esthlos*, which
in general denotes a thing good of its kind and, when applied to human beings, may mean
morally good, brave, or stout; see also *Protagoras* 339c and following.

112. Quoted also in Xenophon's *Symposium* (2.4) and *Memorabilia* (1.2.20); see J. Mitscher-
ling, "Xenophon and Plato," *Classical Quarterly*, n.s., 32 (1982): 468–69.

96a   If he is obedient to sober words.[113] But by teaching
You will never make the bad man good.
Are you considering that he is contradicting himself concerning the same things?

MENO: It appears so.

SOCRATES: Can you state any other matter whatever, then, in which, on the one hand, those who claim to be teachers of it are not agreed to be teachers of others nor even to know it themselves but *are* agreed
96b   to be worthless concerning that very matter they assert they are teachers of; and in which, on the other hand, those who are themselves agreed to be noble and good assert at one time that it is something teachable, at another that it is not? Would you assert that those who are so confused about anything whatever are teachers in the strict sense?

MENO: By Zeus, no—at least I wouldn't!

SOCRATES: Then if neither the sophists nor the noble and good themselves are teachers of the matter, is it clear that no others would be either?

MENO: No others would be, in my opinion.

96c   SOCRATES: And if no teachers, neither are there students?

MENO: In my opinion it is as you say.

SOCRATES: And have we agreed, at least, that in a matter of which there are neither teachers nor students, it isn't something teachable?

MENO: We have agreed.

SOCRATES: So there don't appear to be teachers of virtue anywhere?

MENO: That is so.

SOCRATES: And if no teachers, neither are there students?

MENO: It appears so.

SOCRATES: Virtue, then, wouldn't be something teachable?

96d   MENO: It's not likely, if in fact we've examined it correctly. As a result I really do wonder, Socrates, whether there aren't any good men at all, or [if there are] in what way would they become good.

SOCRATES: We, Meno, are likely to be pretty paltry men, you and I: Gorgias likely hasn't educated you adequately, or Prodicus me. So, more than anything else, we must pay attention to ourselves and inquire into who will make us better, in one way or another. I say these
96e   things with a view to the recent inquiry—how ridiculously it escaped

113. Or, perhaps, "If he is persuaded by moderate myths" (*mythoisi saophrosin*).

our notice that it isn't only when knowledge guides that affairs are carried out correctly and well by human beings; in this way too, perhaps, the knowledge of how in the world good men come to be eludes us.

MENO: How do you mean that, Socrates?

SOCRATES: As follows: that good men must be advantageous—to this, at least, we've correctly agreed that it could not be otherwise. Is that so?

MENO: Yes.

SOCRATES: And that they will be advantageous, if they correctly guide our affairs—to this too, I suppose, we were nobly agreeing?

MENO: Yes.

SOCRATES: But that it is not possible to guide correctly, if one isn't prudent—in this we are like those who've agreed incorrectly.

MENO: How do you mean "correctly"?[114]

SOCRATES: I'll tell you. If someone who knows the path to Larissa (or to anywhere else you like) should walk there and lead others, surely he would lead correctly and well?

MENO: Certainly.

SOCRATES: And what if someone opines correctly what the path is, though he's never been and doesn't know it at all—wouldn't he too guide correctly?

MENO: Certainly.

SOCRATES: And at least for so long, I suppose, as he holds a correct opinion about the things the other fellow has knowledge of, he will be no worse a guide—even though he supposes what is true and has no prudent knowledge[115] of it—than the one who does have prudent knowledge of this.

MENO: For he wouldn't be [any worse].

SOCRATES: True opinion, then, is no worse a guide with a view to correctness of action than is prudence. And this is what we were just now leaving out in the examination of what sort of a thing virtue is, in saying that prudence alone guides acting correctly, whereas there was in fact true opinion too.

MENO: It seems so, at least.

SOCRATES: Correct opinion, then, is no less advantageous than knowledge.

114. The reading of the mss. The adverb is deleted by Burnet and Bluck, following Schanz, but defended by Klein, *Commentary*, 243 n. 5.
115. A verb linked with the noun "prudence" (*phronēsis*); see n. 68.

MENO: But it is less so at least to this extent, Socrates: the one who has knowledge would always hit the mark, but the one with correct opinion sometimes would and sometimes wouldn't hit it.

SOCRATES: How do you mean? Wouldn't the one who always has correct opinion always hit the mark, for so long as he should opine what's correct?

MENO: That appears necessary to me. As a result, Socrates, I wonder, 97d this being so, why in the world knowledge is much more honored than correct opinion, and on account of what the one differs from the other.

SOCRATES: Well, do you know on account of what you are wondering about this, or am I to tell you?

MENO: Say, by all means.

SOCRATES: Because you haven't paid attention to the statues of Daedalus.[116] But perhaps there aren't any in your parts.

MENO: And in reference to what do you say this?

SOCRATES: Because these things too, if they haven't been tied down, escape and run away, but if tied down they stay put.

97e MENO: So, what then?

SOCRATES: To possess one of his creations that's been untied isn't worth a very high price—just like a fugitive slave—for it doesn't stay put, but one that's been tied down is worth much: the works are very beautiful.[117]

In reference to what, then, do I say these things? In reference to the true opinions. For the true opinions too, for so long as they stay put, are a noble thing and accomplish all [manner of] good things. Yet 98a they aren't willing to stay put for a long time but run away from the soul of a human being such that they aren't worth much until someone ties them down by means of a calculation of cause.[118] This, Meno, my comrade, is recollection, as was agreed to by us in what came previously. And once tied down, they first become knowledge,[119] then permanent.[120] On account of these things in particular, knowledge is

116. A legendary sculptor and inventor whose works were said to come alive; see, e.g., *Euthyphro* 11c.
117. Or, "noble" (*kala*). The word translated as "works" (*erga*) is related to the verb translated as "accomplish" in the next paragraph.
118. *Aitia*: see n. 7.
119. Plural in the Greek.
120. Or, "lasting," "stable." The adjective, used substantively here, is related to the verb *menō* (see n. 66).

indeed more honored than correct opinion, and knowledge differs from correct opinion because of the tie.

MENO: By Zeus, Socrates, it's likely to be some such thing.

98b SOCRATES: And yet I too speak as one who doesn't know but is conjecturing. But that correct opinion is something different from knowledge, I'm really *not* of the opinion that I'm just conjecturing. Rather, if in fact I would assert that I know anything—and I would assert it about few things—this, at least, is one thing that I would place among those that I know.

MENO: And what you say is correct, Socrates.

SOCRATES: What then? Isn't the following correct, that when true opinion guides, the task belonging to each action is completed no worse than when knowledge guides?

MENO: Here again what you say is true, in my opinion.

98c SOCRATES: Then correct opinion will be no worse than knowledge nor less advantageous with a view to actions, nor will a man with correct opinion be worse than one with knowledge.

MENO: That is so.

SOCRATES: And yet the good man, at least, was agreed to by us to be advantageous.[121]

MENO: Yes.

SOCRATES: Well, then, since men would be good as well as advantageous to the cities (if in fact they would be) not only through knowledge but also through correct opinion, and since human beings possess neither of these two by nature—neither knowledge nor true

98d opinion nor acquired opinion[122]—or is it your opinion that either of these two is by nature?[123]

MENO: Not in mine, at least.

SOCRATES: Then since they're not by nature, neither would the good be by nature.

MENO: No indeed.

---

121. Or, perhaps, "And yet the good man, at least, was agreed to be advantageous for us."
122. Reading the suggestion of Christopher Bruell, *[doxa] epiktētos,* by which Socrates means to indicate that true opinion "is not acquired but is present somehow by nature" (see *On the Socratic Education: An Introduction to the Shorter Platonic Dialogues* [Lanham, Md.: Rowman & Littlefield, 1999], 179). The text is corrupt, and several editors, including Schanz, Croiset, and Bluck, simply delete the controversial phrase. The reading of three mss., defended by Klein, *Commentary,* 251 n. 26, makes for difficult sense: "and since human beings possess neither of these two by nature—neither knowledge nor true opinion, and [since] neither are they acquired."
123. Socrates does not state the main clause of his sentence.

SOCRATES: And since they're not by nature, we began to examine what came next, whether it is something teachable.

MENO: Yes.

SOCRATES: Did it seem[124] to be something teachable, if virtue is prudence?

MENO: Yes.

SOCRATES: And if it should be something teachable, did it seem that it would be prudence?

MENO: Certainly.

98e SOCRATES: And if there should be teachers of it, did it seem that it would be something teachable, but if not, that it wouldn't be something teachable?

MENO: It did seem so.

SOCRATES: But surely we've agreed that there aren't teachers of it?

MENO: That is so.

SOCRATES: Have we agreed then that it is neither something teachable nor prudence?

MENO: Certainly.

SOCRATES: But surely we agree that it is *good*?

MENO: Yes.

SOCRATES: And that that which guides correctly is advantageous and good?

MENO: Certainly.

99a SOCRATES: And that only these two things guide correctly, true opinion and knowledge, which a human being who guides correctly has—for what happens[125] from chance doesn't happen through human guidance. As for that which a human being has who guides toward what is correct, they are two:[126] true opinion and knowledge.

MENO: So it is, in my opinion.

SOCRATES: Since, then, it isn't something teachable, does virtue no longer come to be through knowledge?[127]

---

124. Or, "Was it opined to be" (*dokein*), here and in the following exchanges, in which the verb is implied.

125. One ms. reads, "what happens correctly from some chance."

126. The reading of the majority of the mss. Some editors, following one ms., alter the text to read in translation: "the things in which a human being guides correctly [are guided by] these two things."

127. The reading of the majority of the mss., according to the *apparatus criticus* of Sharples; Croiset and Burnet adopt a reading that would translate, "Since, then, it isn't something teachable, virtue no longer becomes [is] knowledge?"

MENO: It appears not.

99b SOCRATES: Of the two things that are good and advantageous, then, one has been done away with, and knowledge would not be a guide in political action.

MENO: No, not in my opinion.

SOCRATES: Then it was not by a certain wisdom nor because they were wise that such men—Themistocles and those associated with him, whom Anytus here was just speaking of—used to guide the cities. And so they aren't able to make others such as they themselves are, because they aren't such through knowledge.

MENO: It is likely to be as you say, Socrates.

SOCRATES: Then if not by means of knowledge, what surely remains
99c is that it comes into being by means of good opinion.[128] By using this, the political men guide their cities aright and are no different, when it comes to being prudent, from the soothsayers and divine prophets. For these too say many true things while in an inspired state,[129] but they know nothing of what they say.

MENO: It's likely to be so.

SOCRATES: Is it proper, then, Meno, to call those men "divine" who, though they don't possess intellect, succeed at many great things in what they do and say?

MENO: Certainly.

SOCRATES: So we would correctly call "divine" also those whom we
99d were speaking of just now, soothsayers and prophets and all those skilled at poetry. And we might assert that the political men are, above all these, both divine and inspired, being breathed upon and possessed by the god when they succeed by speaking about many great matters, though they know nothing of what they say.

MENO: Certainly.

SOCRATES: Doubtless women too, Meno, call the good men divine, and the Lacedaemonians say, whenever they praise some good man, "A divine man is he."[130]

99e MENO: And they appear, at least, Socrates, to speak correctly. Yet perhaps Anytus here is annoyed by what you are saying.

---

128. The word (*eudoksia*) is related to the word for opinion (*doxa*) and is often translated as "good repute"; it occurs only here in the dialogue. For a defense of the translation in the text, see Klein, *Commentary,* 253–54; consider also Bruell, *Socratic Education,* 185.
129. The phrase "while in an inspired state" (*enthousiōntes*) is present in only one ms.
130. See Aristotle, *Nicomachean Ethics* 1145a29.

SOCRATES: I, at any rate, don't care.[131] With him, Meno, we will converse again another time. But for now, if we inquired and were speaking nobly in this account as a whole, virtue would be neither by nature nor something teachable but present, in those in whom it is
100a   present, by divine allotment without intellect, unless someone should be that sort of political man able to make another skilled in politics as well. If so, it might almost be said that he would be of such a sort among the living as Homer asserted Teiresias was among the dead, saying about him that,

> He alone among those in Hades is in possession of his senses, but the
> others, as shadows, dart about.[132]

In the same way, such a one would evidently[133] be, in regard to virtue, like a true substance[134] in comparison with shadows.

100b   MENO: In my opinion you speak very beautifully, Socrates.

SOCRATES: Well, on the basis of this calculation, Meno, it's manifest to us that virtue comes to be present, in those in whom it is present, by divine allotment. But we will have clear knowledge about it when we attempt to inquire into what in the world virtue is itself by itself, before inquiring into what way virtue comes to be present in human beings.

But now it's time for me to be off somewhere. As for you, persuade Anytus here, your guest-friend, of the same things that you yourself have been persuaded of, so that he may be gentler. If you do persuade
100c   him, there is a certain benefit you'll render to the Athenians as well.

---

131. R. G. Bury (*Classical Quarterly* 51 [1937]: 119) suggests that these words be given to Anytus on the grounds that they would otherwise be too rude, but all the mss. attribute the remark to Socrates, an attribution defended by Verdenius (ad loc.).

132. Compare Homer, *Odyssey* 10.494–95.

133. The reading (*euthus*) of the majority of mss., defended by Verdenius, whose translation I follow. Burnet follows the reading of one ms. (*enthade*) that would translate: "In the same way, such a one here would be, in regard to virtue, like a true substance."

134. *Pragma*, elsewhere translated, "matter" (see n. 13).

On the *Meno*

The subject matter of the *Meno* is virtue or excellence (*aretē*). The *Meno* can even lay claim to being *the* Platonic dialogue on virtue, for although Plato treats the several virtues at length elsewhere—justice in the *Laws, Republic,* and *Gorgias*; courage in the *Laches* and *Protagoras*; moderation in the *Charmides*; piety in the *Euthyphro*—only in the *Meno* does he raise and pursue the comprehensive question "What is virtue?".

But the next most striking feature of the dialogue is surely the resistance that Socrates meets with throughout in attempting to answer this question. In the first and longest part of the dialogue (70a1–89e5), Socrates must exhort Meno on five occasions to define virtue or to investigate together with him what in the world virtue itself is (71d4–8; 73c6–8; 77a5–b1; 79e5–6; 86c4–6). And even after Socrates rescues Meno from the frustration he succumbs to when brought to see the inadequacy of each of his three definitions of virtue (71e1–72a5; 73c9–d1; 77b1–4), Meno still prefers to investigate the lesser or subsequent difficulty of how virtue is acquired; he remains resistant to Socrates' guiding question to the very end (86c7–d2; 100b4–6). If the root of his ultimate resistance to this question is his now-manifest confusion—as distinguished from his initial resistance or indifference, which stemmed from his conviction that it is "not difficult" to answer it (71e1–2)—we must then wonder what it is that prevents Meno from taking the step that Socrates insists is necessary to clearing up this confusion (e.g., 79d6–e2). Moreover, in the brief but highly charged appearance of the democratic statesman Anytus that constitutes the dialogue's second part (89e6–95a1), Socrates encounters not merely resistance to his general line of inquiry but open hostility.

Finally, in the last part of the dialogue (95a2–100c2), in which Meno returns as Socrates' interlocutor but at which Anytus is present as a silent witness (consider 99e2 and 100b8), Socrates' charge to Meno to persuade Anytus of the things that he himself has been persuaded of proves to be all but impossible: newly equipped with certain "correct opinions" that as such tend to flee those who hold them (97e6–98a3), Meno is probably incapable of persuading Anytus of anything, let alone of making him "gentler" (100c1). And Socrates, for his part, knows full well that he will have occasion to converse with Anytus later on (99e3–4), as of course he did at his trial. The resistance of Meno and that of Anytus combine to prevent Socrates from treating the question "What is virtue?" as he wishes and so to make of the *Meno* an apparently "aporetic" dialogue.

We can begin to discern the source of this resistance by noting that Plato chose as Socrates' principal interlocutors in *the* dialogue on virtue a future political criminal and a future accuser of Socrates: Meno, Socrates' pupil in virtue, will become, a year or so after the dialogue takes place, a spectacular example of political vice (Xenophon, *Anabasis of Cyrus* 2.6.21–29), just as Anytus, Socrates' authority on virtue (89e9–90b6), will shortly thereafter become one of the three Athenian citizens who bring about Socrates' conviction on charges of impiety and corrupting the young and therewith his execution (*Apology of Socrates* 18b3 and context). If Plato's choice of interlocutors was not a frivolous one, we are meant to learn from it; and it leads us to suspect that this very political setting is somehow the appropriate one for investigating the question "What is virtue?" or that this apparently "epistemological" question is (also) a thoroughly political one.

As for the subsequent question of the teachability of virtue, Socrates and Meno eventually arrive at not one but two answers to it: that virtue is knowledge or prudence and hence teachable; and that virtue is not knowledge but a kind of correct opinion given by divine dispensation and hence not teachable. As we shall see, each answer responds to or makes explicit the two different principles present in Meno's opinions about virtue—to the effect that virtue is the carrying out of one's duty or task *and* that it is one's own greatest good or happiness. The elusive unity of the class "virtue," which Meno and Socrates seek, will be uncontroversial only if one's proper tasks or duties are identical to the requirements of one's own greatest good. Plato does all he can, in part through the drama of the dialogue, to indicate how controversial a question this is.

MENO'S THREE ATTEMPTS TO DEFINE VIRTUE

The dialogue begins abruptly with Meno's barrage of questions (70a1–4): "Can you tell me, Socrates, whether virtue is something teachable? Or whether it isn't something teachable but is rather something that can be acquired by practice? Or whether it isn't something that can be acquired by practice or learning, but is present in human beings by nature or in some other way?"

The abruptness and relative complexity of Meno's query imply both an urgent desire to know the answer to it and some prior reflection on it. As for the latter, we discover eventually that Meno believes he shares Gorgias' opinions about virtue (71d1–3) and that Gorgias himself, far from claiming to teach virtue, ridicules those others (the sophists) who do make that claim (95c1–4). When the dialogue opens, then, Meno must at a minimum incline to the view that virtue cannot be taught, and this helps to explain the order of the alternatives he lists: first things first. And yet the very eagerness of his question suggests that he has not settled the matter to his own satisfaction (consider also 95c7–8), as is confirmed by the fact that Socrates leads him to accept, for a time at least, the view that virtue *can* be taught (89c2–4).

Because Socrates professes utter ignorance of "what in the world virtue itself is" and hence also of what sort of a thing it may be, a profession Meno greets with something close to incredulity (71b9–c2), it falls to Meno to offer the first definition of virtue: the virtue of a man is to be capable of carrying out the affairs of the city and, in doing so, to benefit friends, harm enemies, and take care that he himself not suffer any such thing, just as the virtue of a woman is to be able to manage the household well, both preserving its contents and being obedient to the husband. One could state in this way also the virtue of children, male and female, as well as of slaves and freemen, as Meno indicates. And contrary to the impression that Socrates' response leaves (72a6–b7 and c6–d1), Meno does offer, in addition to this enumeration of virtues, a definition meant to encompass them all: "There are also very many other virtues, so there's no perplexity in speaking about what virtue is. For the virtue belonging to each of us is related to each task appropriate to each action and time of life."

Central to Meno's definition of virtue is the "task" ("work," "duty": *ergon*) assigned to each, the demands of the task in question determining the specific content or character of virtue in each case. The many and varied virtues properly share a single "form" (72c7; 72d8 and e5) or constitute a single class because each permits its possessor to contribute directly or indirectly to one and the same goal, the well-being of the city. For if the will of the husband and the needs of the household together determine the virtue of the wife, what else but the will and needs of the city itself could determine the "task" and therewith the virtue of the man, charged as he is with tending to its affairs? Socrates himself, in the course of criticizing this account of virtue, draws attention to its political character by comparing it to a "hive" (or "swarm") of bees. And if Meno had answered the question of what it is that unites the many and varied bees, as he says he could do (72c1–5), he might have parried Socrates' criticism: as the various bees form a class because they are the beings that live in and contribute to the well-being of the hive, so the various virtues form a class because they are the dispositions of soul leading each of us to contribute to the well-being of our political community.

This thoroughly political definition of virtue, approved of for all practical purposes by Aristotle in his *Politics* (1260a25–28 and context), leaves unclear whether the virtues in question are good also for the virtuous themselves. For if the virtuous man must see to it that he not suffer such harm as he may inflict on his enemies, will he also benefit himself as he is to benefit his friends (71e3–5)? Socrates points to this difficulty by speaking no longer of the hive but of the health and strength of the individual man and woman (72d4–73a3): if virtue is determined by our "task," does not the performance of that task promise to be or to lead to our own well-being too? Does not virtue constitute the health and strength (of soul) of the virtuous? Virtue—justice and moderation, for example (73a9, b1–2)— seems to be the necessary means to carrying out the "task" peculiar to us as men or women, elders or children, and therefore to be the necessary means to our becoming good—to our becoming good, that is, not only as husbands or wives, elders or children, but as "human beings" (73a6–c5, noting especially 73b4, b6, and c1–3).

Meno demurs: the case of the virtue of man and woman, on the one hand, and that of their health, on the other, seem "somehow" dissimilar to him (73a4–5). In his first definition of virtue, then, Meno emphasizes the capacity needed to serve well a whole greater than oneself, and he may even harbor some doubt as to whether such service is good for the servant as well. But when prompted to fall once again under the influence of Gorgias (compare 73c6–8 with 71d4), Meno attempts to fulfill (more) directly the promise of virtue to be good for the virtuous themselves. Virtue, he contends, is the capacity to rule human beings, ruling being a very great good for those who do so (as he later makes clear: 78c6–9). The sought-for unity of virtue is here purchased at the price of excluding from the category all but the virtue of the man, as Socrates easily demonstrates by speaking now of the one example that Meno had mentioned in his first definition but that Socrates had thus far omitted, that of the slave (compare 71e1–72a1 with 72d4–6 and 73a2): the virtue of the slave surely cannot be to rule others! Meno could have saved this second or amended definition by contending that the slave equipped with the capacity to rule would indeed be a poor slave but a virtuous human being nonetheless or for that very reason; he might have contended or conceded that a "virtuous" (= dutiful) slave is not a virtuous (= good) human being. But far from defending virtue understood as ruling, Meno is led by Socrates to abandon it immediately: since only just rule is virtuous—because "justice, Socrates, *is* virtue" (73d9–10)—the virtuous human being would rule only when justice permits or requires it. Virtue thus is or results in the attainment of the truly greatest good for oneself at the same time that it (in the form of justice, if not also moderation: compare 73d9–10 with 73a9–b2) may demand the sacrifice of that very good. In this way "virtue" comes to sight as both that which conduces to one's own good *and* that which may call for the sacrifice of one's own good. Ruling others is virtue (73c9), and justice is virtue (73d9–10). Or, to put Meno's confusion another way, he contends that justice is both the whole of virtue and (merely) a part of virtue.

In his eagerness to advance their inquiry, Socrates proceeds to discuss the nature of definition so as to supply a model or models for Meno to follow in speaking about virtue (75a8–9, b4, b11–c1; 77a5–b1). Socrates eventually raises two questions parallel to that pertaining to virtue: "What is shape?" and "What is color?" In taking up the first, Socrates pays close attention to what Meno says about shape or how he "names" or "calls" the various shapes (74d5–6 and d8, e11): we call the round a shape, not shape simply, just as we call the straight a shape, not shape simply; round and straight are in a sense opposites but nonetheless equally fall under the heading "shape." Why is this? Here Socrates is forced to state his own view: shape is that which "alone among the beings happens always to accompany color" (75b9–11). Socrates' definition sticks very close indeed to our ordinary experience of things, for we are somehow aware of both shape and color—the names for each are not meaningless sounds to us—even though we may be unable to state precisely what each is or to define the class character of each; and Socrates' definition serves to clarify the one by means of the other, i.e., to clarify the relation present in our ordinary experience of the two but of which we are not altogether aware. To understand the thing we call "virtue," then, we must make clear to ourselves the elements of it present in our ordinary experience, the interrelation of which elements may not be entirely evident to us.

In the third and last of his definitions, Meno attempts to resolve the tension present in his second, and in doing so he makes clearer still the conflicting principles that guide his conception of the class "virtue." Relying on the authority not of Gorgias but of an unnamed poet, Meno contends that virtue is the capacity of one who desires "the noble [beautiful] things" to provide them for himself (77b2–5). As was evident also from his second definition, Meno himself strongly prefers the noble things to their ignoble counterparts, for he is willing to sacrifice what he understands to be his own good for the sake of what the noble course (e.g., justice) demands. But on what does that willingness rest? Socrates will soon restate the definition in question, with Meno's hearty approval, as "the capacity to provide the good things for oneself" (78c1; also c4–5). He earns the right to do so in part by establishing immediately that Meno understands the noble things to be superlatively good (77b6–7): although there may be goods that are not noble, all noble things—just rule, for example—are indeed good. That is, we surely desire the noble things because, as noble, they are somehow attractive in and of themselves. Yet we also believe them to be good, which means in the context "good for us," as Socrates makes clear. For by maintaining that there is no one who wants to be wretched and unhappy, he corrects Meno's impression that there are some who desire bad things even though they know or suppose them to be bad: insofar as we desire bad things, we do so only on the mistaken assumption that they are good, and we desire the noble things because we believe them to be good and hence conducive to our happiness. Moreover, since all equally want to be happy or to possess for themselves the (truly) good things, and since virtue does not belong to all equally, virtue must consist in the capacity to attain those very things and not in the mere wanting of or wish for them (78b3–c2; note Socrates' approval at 78c3–4).

As Socrates and Meno interpret it, then, this third definition of virtue resolves the tension present in the second by making explicit the hope that guides Meno in his attachment to "the noble things": he hopes to be profoundly benefited thereby. Such "sacrifice" as nobility or virtue demands, then, is, properly speaking, no sacrifice at all. Moreover, the priority of the good to the noble that this account of virtue implies suggests in turn that if a given action could be shown not to be good for one, then neither could it be noble; and precisely one who is most devoted to the noble things should as a result be willing and even eager to forgo it. It remains for Socrates to determine how much of this Meno understands or accepts.

Since virtue is now the capacity "to provide the good things for oneself," acting virtuously should amount to securing health and wealth for oneself, as well as honors in a city and offices—the only sorts of things that are good according to Meno (78c6–7). But Meno cannot abide by this understanding of virtue. To the contrary, Socrates quickly and easily leads him to the view that justice and piety—the latter being mentioned here for the first time (compare 74a4–6)—sometimes demand that we decline such good things. Virtue consists in sometimes providing oneself (or, now, another: 78e5) with gold and silver and sometimes not providing them, depending on the demands of justice. But, to repeat, Meno also believes that the very sacrifice of things good for him will, as a noble act, somehow also be good for him. Meno is even more attracted to the noble sacrifice of the things that he holds to be good for him than he is to the direct attainment of them, but he is so ultimately on the ground that such "sacrifice" of them is advantageous. Socrates concludes this argument by insisting that for so long as the class "virtue" remains unclear, it is impossible to state what its parts are, justice included (consider 79a3–5, b2, and c8–9). In his present condition, Meno has no basis on which to suppose that even justice is a virtue (consider also 71b1–3).

MENO'S REBELLION

When Socrates attempts for the fourth time to elicit from Meno a definition of virtue, this time recurring to the authority of Gorgias, Meno rebels (79e5–80d8). That is, after he playfully compares the effect of conversing with Socrates to that of being numbed by a stingray—and making clear in the process how politically dangerous Socrates' characteristic activity is (80b4–6)—Meno states his famous "paradox" (80d5–8): "By setting out for yourself what sort of a thing, from among those that you don't know, will you make your inquiry? Or even if you happen right upon it, how will you know that this is that thing which you didn't know?" Meno now seems doomed to remain at a loss concerning virtue; so frustrated is Meno by now that he even despairs of rational inquiry altogether.

Perhaps taking his cue from the previous day's conversation (76e8–9), and certainly from their most recent inquiry (78d4, e1), Socrates now conducts an experiment by having recourse to an argument of a very different kind: "I have heard both men and women wise in divine matters—." And with this he hits home, for Meno interrupts him in mid-sentence: "Stating what account [*logos*]?" The wise *logos* in question proves to have two different sources: it is stated both by those of the priests and priestesses who have been concerned with giving a *logos* of the matters in their purview, and by Pindar and all the many other poets who are divine. If perhaps for different reasons, then, the teaching in question is sanctioned by both reason and divine inspiration. According to it, the human soul is immortal and never perishes, "dying" being a misnomer for what is in fact the continual regeneration of the soul. (We note in passing that, in contrast to what we discerned in Socrates' discussion of shape and color, the world of experience as captured by our speech is now and in this crucial respect misleading; reality properly so-called lies beyond or behind the apparent one, the one given in and through ordinary speech.) And from this *logos* concerning the immortality of the soul, Socrates concludes that we must live out our lives as piously as possible because great rewards are available to those who do so: it is through the actions of Persephone that "glorious kings / And men swift in strength and greatest in wisdom" arise, men whose reputations remain unsullied for the rest of time. Socrates thus paints a vivid and alluring picture of the rewards—among them reputation and strength and rule—that await the politically ambitious Meno if only he will remain true to his (repeatedly demonstrated) inclination to forgo the direct pursuit of what he holds to be his own greatest good for the sake of or in the name of nobility, of justice in particular.

And yet, for all of Meno's interest in it, this part of Socrates' report does nothing to alleviate Meno's disheartened condition; the exhortation to live as piously as possible does not establish the possibility of attaining knowledge of virtue. What then is its purpose? We recall that, at the core of Meno's eagerness to sacrifice his own good lies his desire to obtain precisely the good things for himself; insofar as Meno believes that he can attain the truly good things for himself only by being willing to sacrifice them (in the name of justice or piety), Socrates can strengthen Meno's attachment to justice, and hence his self-restraint here and now, by encouraging him in his belief that such sacrifice is indeed ultimately good for him. For if this world is not such that the noble (= self-sacrificing) are always rewarded for their nobility, let alone rewarded with great power and reputation, it would be salutary to posit a different world, a subsequent life or lives, in which the noble will receive their just deserts through divine intervention.

But this leaves unexplained the root of Meno's prior attachment to justice (or nobility); why is Meno more attracted in the first place to such goods as he believes are available to him through the sacrifice of the good things, than he is to the direct attainment of them? Socrates' introduction in this context of Persephone's rewards in the next life or lives, and of the prospect of undying reputation, suggests that the root in question is bound up with the desire for immortality: Meno's deepest wish, one may venture to say, is not only to possess for himself the good things, but to possess them for himself always. And because Meno performed poorly on the earlier test meant to determine the extent of his self-knowledge, and in particular his awareness of the nature of his attraction to the good things, Socrates now has recourse to the view of the world made necessary by Meno's confusion and, to that extent, sanctioned by reason itself.

If Socrates' report concerning the rewards of Persephone does not directly assuage Meno's distress concerning the possibility of knowledge, his explanation of the consequences of the soul's immortality is certainly intended to do so. For the immortal soul has seen all things, both those in Hades and those here, and it is not possible for it not to have learned all things at some time. It is nothing to be wondered at, then, if the soul can be made to recollect the things that it once knew, provided it recalls some one thing first (81d2). Since our souls have already learned what virtue is, we need only recollect here and now the knowledge that is present but dormant in us. Thus what is called "learning" is but recollection, properly speaking. (In this important case too, how human beings speak of things is deceptive.)

After this brief series of assertions, which Socrates merely "trusts" to be true (81e1–2), he is ready to return to the question of what virtue is. Meno is not. And yet he challenges only the equation of learning with recollection—that is, he is willing to let stand Socrates' report concerning the immortality of the soul and the rewards of Persephone. This willingness is an important demonstration of the connection between Meno's state of soul and the "providential" view of the world he readily adopts or confirms. Convinced both that political power is the greatest good for himself and that it is noble sometimes to sacrifice the attainment of it, because doing so is superlatively good for him, Meno fails to see what it is that he truly wants. The selflessness he is attracted to for selfish reasons renders him open to and indeed eager for the services of Persephone.

Socrates' lengthy response to Meno's paradox includes his celebrated conversation with one of Meno's slaves, the avowed purpose of which is to demonstrate the proposition that all learning is but recollection of knowledge gained in a previous life or lives. In three successive stages, Socrates poses geometrical puzzles for the slave to solve, despite or rather because of the fact that the slave has never been taught geometry; the correct answers the slave comes up with must therefore have a source other than knowledge acquired in this life. But on the basis of these exchanges, we conclude that the process of "recollection" is a difficult one, for the slave performs poorly under Socrates' questioning. In fact, Socrates himself leads the slave to the correct answers eventually, answers arrived at by performing simple acts of calculation, of putting two and two together (82d4). Attractive as these passages may be to us, they do not prove that all learning is recollection, still less that all can recollect equally; they establish only that the slave understands basic concepts of shape, size, and proportion (line, square, double, half) that would be known to anyone having learned a language (consider Socrates' all-important question at 82b4). The slave does not know and never "recollects" the name "diagonal," for example, because this is taught by sophists with whom he has had no contact in this or apparently any other life (85b4).

The arguments concerning recollection are defective in part because they beg the decisive question of the teachability of virtue. Even if the soul has learned "all things," i.e., all things subject to learning, Socrates nowhere proves that virtue is among them. We must not forget that the entire digression with Meno's slave is meant chiefly to alleviate Meno's frustration or despair, and in this it is successful (compare 79e7–80d8 with 86c4–7). That is, it is a rhetorical argument intended to persuade, one that Socrates himself admits he would be unwilling to fight very hard for (86b6–c2). But these exchanges do introduce an important puzzle concerning our knowledge of virtue. For even granting that the soul is immortal, that all nature is akin, and that every soul has—somehow—learned "all things" in a previous life or lives (81c5–d1), it turns out that we not only—somehow—forget the knowledge we have learned but also take on in its stead false opinions. Chief among these false opinions is our conviction that we know something—what virtue is, for example—when in fact we no longer do. And this means that, as there is an ignorance peculiar to our existence here and now, so there is a learning and hence a knowledge peculiar to our existence here and now that cannot itself be an example of recollection—namely, learning and hence coming to know that we do not know that something in fact (for previously we did know it). Moreover, the passage from our present ignorance to our knowledge of that ignorance is effected, according to Socrates, by "questioning" (86a7) of the kind to which he has just subjected both Meno and his slave.

In both cases, Socrates elicits from his interlocutors opinions that are indeed present in them but of which they are not altogether aware; and as he now stresses, some of those opinions are true (86a7), although their truth is hidden in part because they coexist with false counterparts. While it may be quite possible not to know a specific human being and hence his characteristics, it now appears impossible not to have at least opinions, and indeed some true opinions, about virtue: with more justification than he knew, Meno first greeted Socrates' profession of utter ignorance about virtue with incredulity (71a1–c2). What then is the *source* of these opinions in us, true as well as false—if we discount, as indeed we must, Socrates' official (theological-rhetorical) explanation? That the answer to this question involves considerations of politics appears from the remaining sections of the dialogue.

On the Political Character of Virtue

Despite Socrates' suggestion that they continue to pursue the question of what virtue is, Meno insists that they turn instead to the subsequent question of whether it is teachable. Socrates yields but without letting his own question drop entirely: the question of the teachability of virtue will be considered by asking what sort of thing virtue must be, if it is to be teachable (87b2–6). The gist of the argument runs as follows: virtue is good; there is nothing good that is not encompassed or governed by (a kind of) knowledge; virtue is therefore (a kind of) knowledge. But in what sense are all goods encompassed by knowledge, according to Socrates? Such bodily or external goods as health, strength, beauty, and wealth sometimes benefit us and sometimes harm us; only when we make "correct use" of each do they benefit us. This is true even of the things of the soul: what we call moderation, justice, courage, docility, memory, magnificence, and so on benefit us only when they are guided by knowledge, and Socrates here identifies prudence as the knowledge of how to use these so as to benefit ourselves: courage absent prudence is but harmful boldness (88b3–6; compare *Protagoras* 350a6–b6 and context). The standard determining not only the goodness of the external goods but also the goodness and hence the virtuous character of the various "virtues" is their contribution to one's own good: all that issues in one's own happiness (88c3) or is advantageous

(89a2) is governed by prudence; and since virtue is here nothing but the advantageous for oneself, it may be equated with (the whole or a part of) prudence (89a3–4). We have thus returned to an understanding of virtue very close to that seen in Socrates' examination of Meno's third definition.

Socrates concludes from this argument that those who are good would not be such by nature, presumably on the grounds that if virtue is a kind of knowledge or prudence, it is rational and hence acquired through teaching. Yet the evidence Socrates adduces to support this conclusion is puzzling, to say the least: if there were such good persons by nature, the city would have set people to watch over them as soon as they became apparent in order to keep them from being corrupted and to insure that they would become "useful to the cities." There are not overseers of this kind; therefore the good are not by nature (89b1–7; note Meno's somewhat puzzled response). This reference to the *political* utility of the virtuous or good recalls an anomaly in the argument summarized in the preceding paragraph but omitted there: between his assertion that all good things are encompassed by knowledge (87d4–8) and his proof or clarification of it (87e5 and following), Socrates had added that not only would virtue, being good, be advantageous (beneficial), but so too would we be advantageous (beneficial) insofar as we are virtuous (87d8–e2). This latter assertion, which is developed only now and anticipates what is to come (96e7–97a4, 98c5–6, 8–9), compels us to wonder for whom or for what the virtuous are as such advantageous. For although virtue has just been equated with prudence and hence the capacity to benefit oneself or to be happy, it is now that which enables one to be "useful to the cities." We have thus returned to a definition of virtue akin to Meno's first. What is more, as soon as Socrates has introduced (or reintroduced) the idea of virtue as political service, he retracts the premise that virtue is knowledge and hence teachable (89c5 and following).

This drastic change in the argument takes place just before the arrival of Meno's guest-friend, Anytus. As Anytus takes a seat among them, Socrates is in the midst of arguing that virtue is not teachable because teachable things will have both teachers and students of them and, despite his best efforts, he has so far failed to find a teacher of virtue. That the "virtue" now under discussion is very far removed from prudence becomes clear from Socrates' restatement to Anytus of what it is that Meno wishes to possess, a restatement that emphasizes service to others in ways and to a degree that Meno himself had never done: "[Meno] desires that wisdom and virtue by means of which human beings nobly manage both households and cities and tend to their own parents and know how both to receive and to send off citizens and guest-friends in a manner worthy of a good man" (91a2–6). Socrates then retreats from his contention that there are no teachers of virtue just long enough to test Anytus' reaction to the possibility that the proper teachers of virtue are the sophists, who after all claim to teach it and charge a fee for doing so (91b7–8; 95c1–4). The vehemence of Anytus' condemnation of the sophists is matched only by its baselessness, convinced as he is of their pernicious character through no experience of his own or that of his kin. Anytus maintains instead that every Athenian gentleman is a competent teacher of virtue, and he thus belies Socrates' claim at the beginning of the dialogue that all Athenians would "laugh" at the suggestion that they know what virtue is or, therefore, whether it can be taught (compare 71a1–b4 with 92e3–93a4 and 94e3–7). With the dramatic entry of Anytus, just after Socrates has begun the argument meant to deny that (political) virtue is knowledge or prudence, Plato reminds us of how politically charged the inquiry into virtue is and how dangerous or offensive Socrates' apparently modest claims to ignorance are.

If common decency, as one might call the virtue now at issue, can indeed be passed on from elder to youth (93a2–3) and from father to son (95e9–96a2), in one way or another (consider 95e9–96a2 again in the light of *Protagoras* 325b5–326e5), the kind of virtue that Socrates speaks of next—that of the greatest statesmanship embodied by such luminaries as Themistocles, Aristides, Pericles, and Thucydides—clearly cannot be. Even Anytus must admit that these illustrious fathers failed to pass on to those whom they most cared for, their sons, the skill or wisdom for which each is celebrated (93a2–95a1, noting especially the transition from "the noble and good" at 93a2 to "those good at the political things" at 93a5–6). And just as the claim of the sophists to teach virtue was dismissed merely on the basis of Anytus' uninformed prejudice against them, so Socrates here denies the teachability of (political) virtue in *both* senses, the higher and the lower, solely on the grounds that the higher cannot be taught.

Evidently angered by Socrates (consider 94e3–95a1 in light of 99e2), Anytus withdraws from the conversation but not the group (91a2, 6, 92d4–5). As a result, Socrates turns to Meno, but he too is unable to supply evidence that either the gentlemen ("the noble and good") or the sophists can teach virtue. Purportedly to establish that not only do political men like Meno have contradictory opinions on the matter but that even a poet (Theognis) states contradictory things about it, Socrates adduces three quotations, the first dealing with learning from the great or powerful, the second with instilling intellectual understanding or comprehension (*noēma*), the third with fostering such obedience as one gains from listening to a father's moderate words or myths. But Theognis speaks explicitly of teaching (or being taught) only in the first and third quotations (95d6, 96a1). In the case of great statesmanship or power, he contends that one can be taught noble (*esthla*) things by being with the powerful and being pleasing to them, and in the case of ordinary decency, by contrast, he speaks of the effectiveness of obedience as distinguished from teaching: Theognis may not in fact contradict himself.

Theognis' lines are important in part because they summarize the different understandings of "virtue" present in the *Meno*: political virtue understood as either common decency or great statesmanship, which Socrates insists is not teachable; and virtue proper, which is (a kind of) knowledge or prudence and is as such teachable. And in the person of Anytus, Plato puts before our eyes a living embodiment of political virtue, certainly in its lesser form but also, as Anytus himself apparently believes (95a4), in its higher form. As for the source of his opinions about virtue, no recourse to an immortal soul or to Persephone is needed to discover it, for he has come to hold the opinions he does as a result of the rearing and education given him in this life by his father, Anthemion (90b1; consider also 95e9–96a2), a self-made man noteworthy for his modesty as a citizen and his orderliness and good behavior as a man (90a1–b3). Moreover, the correctness of that education and of the opinions thereby instilled in Anytus is confirmed for him in a most powerful way: by the hearty approval of the Athenian multitude, who "elect him to the greatest offices" (90b2–3). Because he has received from earliest youth a most emphatic answer to the question "What is virtue?" Anytus feels no need to raise it himself, let alone to countenance any suggestion that it is the sophists who teach virtue or— still less—that it cannot be taught at all. To affirm either would be to denigrate the paternal education he has received, and his attachment to it or its sources is evidently greater than his attachment to or longing for the truth.

Yet the education characteristic of Anytus is true of us all to some degree. Each of us, that is, is reared in and educated by a specific family that is in turn shaped by a specific political community, and these place their mark on us, on our souls, as surely as Athens and Anthemion did on Anytus. Only by being brought to see the contradictory character of some of our most important opinions can we begin truly to question their adequacy, if our nature is otherwise equipped to do so; only through the kind of "questioning" (86a7) that Socrates has attempted to carry out in the *Meno* can the true but partially obscured opinions that dwell within us be roused and transformed into knowledge, those opinions that are merely "correct" ("orthodoxy") being abandoned in the process (note how carefully Socrates distinguishes between "correct" and "true" opinion: compare 97b1, 5, c4, 7, 9, d2, 98a7, b2, c1–3, 10, d1 with 86a7, 97b9, c2, e6, 98b7, d1, 99a2, 5).[1] Neither Anytus nor Meno proves to be a proper subject of such questioning: the whole of Anytus' life depends on the stability of the answers he has already received; and Meno, though younger and thus having less at stake, proves unable to see or to face up to the nature of his confusion regarding virtue.

The final subsection of the dialogue (96d5–100c2), like Socrates' lengthy reply to Meno's "paradox," clearly serves a rhetorical purpose: it is meant to equip Meno with opinions that may enable him to "persuade" Anytus in turn and so to make him "gentler" (100b8–c2). And as with that earlier reply (86b6–7), Socrates here notes the inadequacy of the argument even as he makes it (100b4–6; compare 98b2–5). Leaving intact the argument that the virtue under discussion is not knowledge and hence not teachable, Socrates adds only that, for those who would guide "our affairs" (97a3–4) or be "advantageous to the cities" (98c9) or guide aright "political action" (99b2), correct opinion, as distinguished from knowledge, is enough. Statesmen know what they are talking about as little as do soothsayers and divine prophets (99c2–3, d1; compare 92c6). But if the source of (true) virtue, being a kind of knowledge, is learning or instruction, what is the source of this "correct opinion" or of the specific virtue in which it issues? According to Socrates, such opinion is granted them through "divine allotment" (99e6, 100b2–3). This answer fills the gap left by Meno's opening question, in which he had spoken of teaching (or learning) and practice, as well as nature and some unnamed fourth possibility (70a1–4). The more obvious candidate might well seem to be *nomos* ("law," "custom"), the opposite of "nature." But *nomos* is conspicuous in the *Meno* by its absence, Plato resorting to paraphrases of it (see 70b6, 76d8, 82a5). Or could it be that if not the word, at any rate its power, is very much present in the dialogue, in which we witness its capacity to shape our opinions about virtue and the particular characteristics of the gods, of the "divine allotment," in a given time and place? At all events, the most that can be said in favor of

---

1. See also Christopher Bruell, "Meno," in *On the Socratic Education: An Introduction to the Shorter Platonic Dialogues* (Lanham, Md.: Rowman & Littlefield, 1999), 184. My own approach to the *Meno* has been aided by this definitive study.

Socrates' new suggestion is that it recalls the intervention of Persephone in granting to those who deserve it great power and strength and (a certain) wisdom (81b8–c4; consider 93e3, 7, 94b1, as well as 90a2 and 91a3): the great statesmen are marked by an understanding that transcends knowledge and that is justly theirs.

Socrates all but ends the dialogue by noting that there may be a sort of politician who *can* make others such as he is and who would thus be to those here as the wise Teiresias was among the mere shades of Hades (100a1–7). This unexpected admission of the possibility of teaching politics would be unintelligible had not Socrates asserted, in the *Gorgias* (a dialogue to which the *Meno* is obviously linked), that he is perhaps alone among the Athenians in undertaking "the true political art" and is alone in carrying out "the political things" (521d6–8): the true political art does what every political community tries but fails to do adequately—namely, to care for the health of our souls. Socrates, of course, is the "political" man in question. Only he understands the needs of the soul and so its proper task; only he understands as a result its specific virtue. And virtue so understood, being rational, is teachable. We are reminded of how far Socrates is from the view of the world with which he had earlier enticed Meno, by the manner in which he now quotes Homer's description of Teiresias (100a2–7): he alters the text (*Odyssey* 10.494–95) so as to suppress the fact that it was Persephone who had bestowed on the great seer his powers. The understanding that Socrates possesses and (to the extent possible) teaches owes nothing to "Persephone."

Appendix
Xenophon's Assessment of Meno
(*Anabasis of Cyrus* 2.6.21–27)

In 401 B.C., Cyrus ("the Younger") sought to wrest the rule of the Persian Empire from his older brother Artaxerxes II (c. 436–358 B.C.), who had come to power following the death of their father, Darius II, in 405 B.C. and who now viewed his younger brother with suspicion. Accordingly, Cyrus amassed a force comprising both his own Persians, under the command of Ariaeus, and Greek mercenaries, the latter including eventually Meno of Thessaly and his comrade Aristippus among the generals and, in a private capacity, Xenophon himself. Cyrus had kept from the generals and soldiers the true purpose of this expedition, however, and revealed it to them only when it could no longer be concealed; in convincing the Greeks to set aside their anger and to follow Cyrus in his rebellion against the king, Meno played a crucial part. Unfortunately, Cyrus was killed in the first major battle, and the Greeks then found themselves in an exceedingly precarious position, being without a plausible claimant to the throne of Persia and hence without a flag to rally around, abandoned in territory both hostile and unknown to them. It was in the midst of this crisis that Meno, together with his Persian friend Ariaeus, betrayed Cyrus' Greek contingent to the king in the hope of winning the favor of the latter. This betrayal resulted in the slaughter of all the Greek generals and several of their captains. What follows is Xenophon's assessment of Meno.

2.6. (21) Meno the Thessalian was clear in his desire to be exceedingly wealthy, in his desire to rule so as to get hold of more, and in his desire to be honored so that he might gain greater profit; he wanted to be a friend to those with the greatest power so that he might not pay a penalty for his injustices. (22) As for accomplishing the objects of his desires, he supposed the shortest path to be through perjury and lying and deception, simplicity and truthfulness being the same as foolishness. (23) Affection he manifestly showed no one, and he clearly became a hostile plotter to precisely whomever he said he was a friend; he ridiculed no enemy, but in conversation he was always ridiculing all his associates. (24) He also did not plot against the possessions of his enemies, for he supposed it to be difficult to get hold of the things of those on their guard; but as for the things of friends, he supposed that he alone knew it to be easiest to get hold of them, since they are unguarded. (25) All those whom he perceived to be perjurers and unjust he was afraid of, on the ground that they were well armed, but those who were pious and made a practice of the truth he tried to use, on the ground that they were lacking in manliness. (26) And just as somebody prides himself on piety and truthfulness and justice, so Meno prided himself on the capacity to deceive, on the concocting of lies, on the mockery of friends. He always held that somebody who was not a scoundrel was among the uneducated; and with those with whom he attempted to be first in friendship, he supposed it necessary, to acquire this, to slander those who were the first in fact. (27) As for supplying himself with obedient soldiers, he contrived this by sharing in their injustices. He thought he deserved to be honored and tended to because he showed that he had the power and the willingness to commit the greatest injustices. He counted it a benefaction done, whenever someone broke with him, that in using him he hadn't destroyed him.

Xenophon concludes his account by noting that Meno was not simply beheaded by the king of Persia, as were the captains and other generals, the manner of execution thought to supply "the quickest death." Instead, "it is said that, after having been tortured alive for one year, he met the end of a wicked man." (2.6.29)